D1584311

iii

introduction

aims

This book is intended for any new user of Windows 3.1, Windows for Workgroups or MS-DOS. It will help the user to make more effective use of a personal computer by providing an understanding of what an operating system is and why we need Windows and MS-DOS. The book assumes no technical knowledge and is suitable for use at college, work or home.

The book covers the most important features of MS-DOS versions 5.0 to 6.22, Windows 3.1 and Windows for Workgroups (3.11).

structure

The purpose of this book is to cover both MS-DOS and Windows 3.1/3.11 in a single reasonably priced volume. As Microsoft, the developer of both, has merged the two operating environments, it makes sense to learn them both together.

The book introduces the features of MS-DOS and Windows in the context of practical activitites to perform or problems to solve. In this way any underlying theory is supported with opportunities for independent practice and consolidation. Each unit is divided into a number of short activities which guide the user step-by-step through the necessary skills. Solutions to selected activities are given at the end of the book.

To complete the MS-DOS activities in the book you will need:

❏ At least two new blank unformatted diskettes or floppy disks (use 1.44 Mb high density disks if possible)

❏ An IBM or compatible personal computer (PC)

a note to lecturers and students

This learning material requires little, if any, input by lecturers, and can therefore be used on programmes based on independent learning. A disk containing the files used in the book is available free to all lecturers adopting the book as a course text.

Jim Muir
1996

iv

what is an operating system, and what is MS-DOS?

At this stage a theoretical definition of an operating system would probably be confusing and unhelpful. However, it is important to realise very early on that the operating system is the software or set of programs which controls the basic actions of your hardware – the keyboard, screen, main memory, disk drive and so on. In addition, the operating system loads and runs application software and manages your data files. It might be helpful to think of the operating system as a bridge between you, your hardware and your programs. It translates your commands into a form that the computer can understand so that you can use the software to do the job you bought it for. And without you realising it, the operating system is working in the background on utility or housekeeping programs: copying or deleting files on disk, backing up the whole disk or checking the hardware.

MS-DOS is an operating system developed by Microsoft. It is not the only operating system but it has become the standard system used on most PCs. This degree of standardisation is of great benefit as it allows software applications to be developed which will run on most PCs.

why do we need both Windows and MS-DOS?

Many users found MS-DOS difficult and unfriendly to use. Commands can be hard to remember and easy to get wrong. The Windows environment makes a great improvement for the non-technical user by providing easily recognisable pictures and icons to represent applications and commands. However, to run a program using Windows 3.11 or earlier will also require the use of MS-DOS, as Windows 3.11 and earlier versions simply provide an interface between the user and the operating system. Windows 95, the most recent version of Windows, does not require MS-DOS as it is an operating system in itself.

Part 1

Windows 3.1 and Windows for Workgroups

Conventions used in Part 1

The terms 'DOS' and 'MS-DOS' are used interchangeably.

The terms 'PC', 'personal computer' and 'computer' are used interchangeably.

Keyboard entries may be typed in lower or upper case. I use upper case for clarity. If you wish to use upper case then use the Caps Lock key.

Unless otherwise stated an activity will work with all versions of Windows 3.1 and Windows for Workgroups.

Diskettes needed

For these activities you will need two suitable three and a half inch high density diskettes, (floppy disks) preferably new ones that do not contain any files. The Format and Delete commands will erase any information on them.

A brand new disk needs to be formatted before it can be used – consult Unit 3, Activity 3 for information on different disk formats if necessary.

unit 1
Windows – the introductory essentials

Introduction

In this unit you will learn such essential preliminaries as starting up Windows, finding your way around the main desktops and menus, using the mouse and opening and closing applications. Don't be tempted to skip these activities if you are fairly new to Windows. They lay the foundation for more advanced skills and they give you a general understanding of what Windows is and how it works.

Skills covered	Activity
Control-menu box – using	2.2
Help – using	3.12
icons – rearranging	3.11
Menus – using	3.7
Mouse actions	2.6
Scrolling	2.5, 3.12
Window – closing	2.2, 3.10
Window – opening	3.10
Window features – using	2
Window – maximising	2.4, 3.9
Window – minimising	2.4, 3.9
Window – restoring	2.4
Window size – changing	2.4
Windows – arranging	3.7

Previous skills required

None

Activity 1   Starting Windows

There are several ways of loading the Windows operating environment, depending on how your computer has been set up. If the first method fails then try the others.

Method 1 Automatic loading

First turn on your computer (and the screen too if necessary)

If the Windows logo appears then Windows is starting. Make a note of the version of Windows on your computer, e.g. Windows 3.1, Windows for Workgroups, as some of the instructions that follow are particular to certain versions.

(If Windows 95 loads then you cannot use this book)

In a few seconds the opening screen, titled Program Manager will appear – see Figure 1.

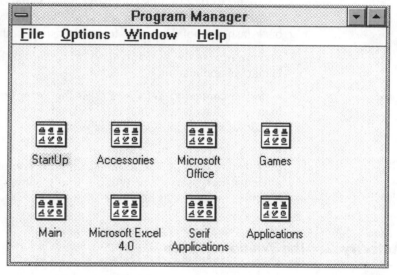

Figure 1

Don't worry if your opening screen is different to this; your computer may have been set up differently. Go on to the next activity now.

Method 2 Starting from a menu

Some PC's, especially those in colleges, display a main menu system when first turned on. Is there a Windows option on the menu? If so take it, e.g. type the option number and press the **Enter** key if necessary. This large L–shaped key is on the right of the keyboard and is marked with a curled arrow.

Now refer to method 1 above to check your Windows version and opening screen.

3

Method 3 Starting from MS-DOS

1. Perhaps all that your PC displays are the symbols C:\> or similar. This is the MS-DOS operating system prompt.

2. Type **WIN** and then press the **Enter** key. This large L-shaped key is on the right of the keyboard and is marked with a curled arrow. If the Windows logo is displayed next then refer to method 1 above to check your Windows version and opening screen.

3. If nothing happens, or you get an error message, then try the following:

    Type the command **DIR/W** and press the **Enter** key.

    A list of names appears; the names in square brackets are the names of directories.

    Identify one called [WINDOWS] or similar.

    Type the command **CD\WINDOWS** and press the **Enter** key. (you will need to modify this command if the name of your directory is different) If you get an error message check that you have used the backslash symbol (\) not the forward slash (/) in the command.

    You are now in the directory (part of the hard disk) that contains the Windows application.

    Type the command **WIN** and press the **Enter** key. If the Windows logo is displayed next then refer to method 1 above to check your Windows version and opening screen.

    If you have tried all three methods and have failed to start Windows then it may well not be installed on your computer – seek expert advice if necessary. You will be able to attempt the DOS-based activities in later units however.

Activity 2 The Windows screen

1. Let's do a quick tour of the Program Manager, the first window to appear when you start Windows. It contains most of the standard Windows features so we will use it to learn the key Windows terms and actions (shown in italic).

2. Study Figure 1 carefully first. It shows a single *window,* the *Program Manager,* with a group of *icons* at the bottom. Icons are pictures or graphic images that represent applications or groups of applications – more about these later.

    The window itself is on a background known as the *desktop* which may be plain or patterned. It is used as a working area to open windows, work with them and close them when no longer needed.

More than one window can be open at a time; you may find that when you start Windows the Program Manager is overlaid by another window or windows.

Figure 2. shows the Program Manager window overlaid by the *Main* window. If this happens then proceed as follows, otherwise skip to section 3.

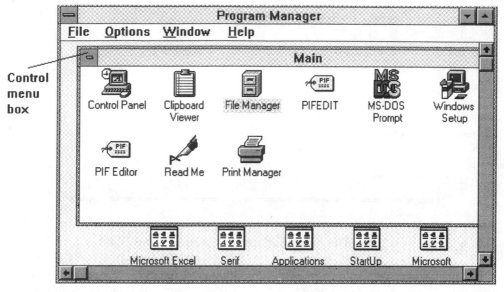

Control menu box

Figure 2

Move the mouse – the *pointer* on the screen moves. Locate the screen pointer on the *Control-menu box* at the top left of the Main window – see Figure 2. There is a similar box on the Program Manager window, do not confuse the two.

Now press the left button on the mouse twice in quick succession.

The Main window is closed, leaving Program Manager open – try again if it doesn't work the first time.

Repeat the above operation for any other window that may overlay the Program Manager window.

Your screen should now resemble Figure 3 below; don't worry if your screen looks different we are just identifying the main features at the moment.

3.   a.   **Title and Title Bar.** Every window has these. Depending on the type of window the title can be the name of an application, a file or as in the case of Program Manager a group of applications. If there are several windows open then the title bar of the *active* window – the one that you are working on – appears as a deeper colour than the others

5

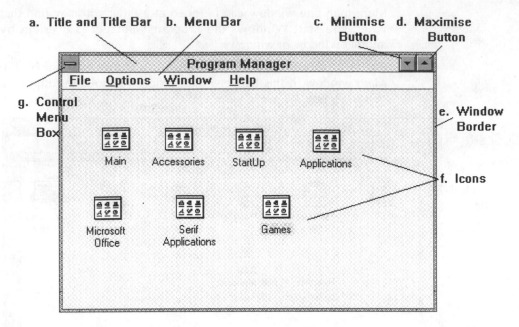

Figure 3

b. **The Menu bar** appears just below the Title Bar and shows a list of options – File, Options, Window and Help. Each option contains a list of commands that you can use in this window. The menu options will vary from one window to another.

c. **The Minimise button** is in the top right hand corner of every window. It allows you to reduce the window to the size of an icon. This is used when you no longer need a window.

d. **The Maximise button** (immediately to the right of the Minimise button) allows you to enlarge the window to the full size of the screen. This gives you more room to work if needed. If the screen is already maximised then the Maximise button is replaced by a double-headed Restore button that restores the window to its previous size – see Figure 5 below.

e. **The Window border** is a double line enclosing each window. The corners of the border are specially marked. The sides and corners of the border can be used to change the size of a window.

f. Icons are small pictures or graphic images. They represent windows which aren't being used at the moment. In the case of Program Manager there are typically four icons – Main, Accessories, Applications and StartUp. – the picture on each of them indicates that they contain further groups of applications that are currently inactive.

g. **The Control-menu box** is in the top left-hand corner of every window. It allows you to close, move and alter the sizes of windows.

6

Now that we've identified some of the basic Windows components, let's try some of them out; keep referring to Figure 3 if necessary.

4. **Window size.** This often causes frustration when you start out; typical problems are a window suddenly disappearing or shrinking in size.

Move the screen pointer onto the **Minimise** button and click the mouse button once. The Program Manager window is minimised to an icon – see Figure 4 below.

Figure 4

Move the screen pointer onto this icon and 'double click', i.e. click the mouse button twice in quick succession. The Program Manager window is restored to its previous size. Try again if you are not successful the first time.

Now click the **Maximise** button once. The window enlarges to fill the entire desktop. The Maximise button is replaced by a double headed **Restore** button – see Figure 5.

Restore Button

Figure 5

Click the Restore button and the window is restored to its previous size.

To make finer size adjustments we must use the window Border. Move the screen pointer to the bottom right-hand border of the window – the screen pointer changes to a double-headed arrow when correctly located.

Now press down the mouse button and keep it pressed down.

Drag the edge of the worksheet diagonally towards the top left of the screen until the window measures about 2 inches square. Then let go.

Your window will now resemble Figure 6.

7

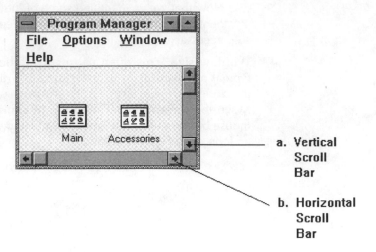

a. Vertical Scroll Bar

b. Horizontal Scroll Bar

Figure 6

Three main changes have taken place:

First the Title and Menu Bars are much shortened – the four menu options have 'wrapped round' in order to fit them in,

Secondly some or all of the icons seem to have disappeared – compare the re-sized window with Figure 3.

Thirdly two new Windows features have appeared – horizontal and vertical scroll bars. if you don't have both sets of scroll bars then make the window even smaller until they appear.

Scroll bars are permanent features of some windows, but with group windows such as Program Manager they will only appear if the window is too small to show all the icons.

5. **Scrolling.** Move the screen pointer onto the down arrow button of the vertical scroll bar (marked a. on figure 6) and hold the mouse button down. The window scrolls, revealing some of the concealed icons

   Now move the screen pointer onto the left arrow button of the horizontal scroll bar and hold down the mouse button as before, the rest of the icons scroll into view.

   Finally restore the window to its previous size – drag the border of the window diagonally to the bottom right of the screen.
   All the icons will be in view again. If so the scroll bars will have disappeared – they are not needed.

6. **Mouse control** You have now learnt the 3 basic mouse actions:

   Clicking – locate screen pointer, press left mouse button once

   Double clicking – locate screen pointer and press left mouse button twice in quick succession

Dragging – locate screen pointer, hold down left button while moving the mouse, release button.

From now on I shall be using these names to refer to these actions.

Activity 3 Moving, opening and closing windows

Confusion often arises when you have more than one window open at once; try out the following tasks.

1. If you are starting a new windows session make sure that only the Program Manager window is open – see Activity 2 above.

2. Enlarge the size of the window if necessary so that all the icons are visible – see Activity 2 above.

3. Now move the screen pointer onto the **Main** icon and double click. The Main window opens, overlaying the Program Manager window.
   A further group of icons are displayed in this second window, representing applications that we shall be using in future units.

   Your screen should resemble Figure 7. Don't worry if the relative positions and sizes of your two windows vary from this.

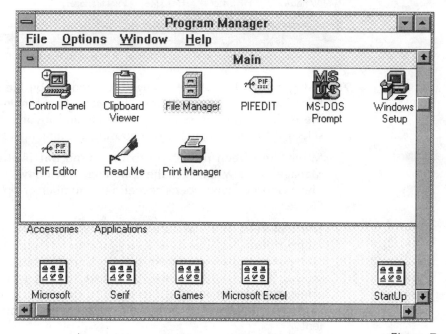

Figure 7

4. Now repeat the above operation for the **Accessories** icon in the Program Manager window– a third window is now opened.

5. It is now easy to see how working with multiple windows can cause confusion; one window overlays another, often hiding the

title and the icons it contains. Let's experiment with moving and re-sizing these windows.

6.   For the purposes of the exercises that follow we will need to make each window fairly small so that they overlay each other. Re-size them (see Activity 2, section 4) so that they resemble Figure 8. It doesn't matter which window is on top for the moment.

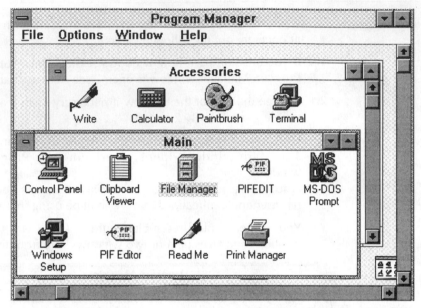

Figure 8

7.   **Using menus.** We can re-arrange the windows on the desktop by selecting some commands from the Menu Bar; a menu choice is the main method of issuing commands and involves two steps, selecting the menu option then choosing a command from it.

Move the screen pointer onto the menu bar in the Program Manager window and click the option name **Window.**
The Window menu opens revealing a number of options – see Figure 9.

Shortcut keys: You will notice that a letter is underlined in each menu option, eg C̲ascade, Tile H̲orizontally etc. This allows commands to be issued from the keyboard, rather than using a mouse. If you hold down the Alt or Ctrl key and type the appropriate letter the command is executed.
In these units we will be using the mouse, not the keyboard equivalent.

Hint: If you open the wrong menu then click the correct menu option or simply click elsewhere on the window to cancel.

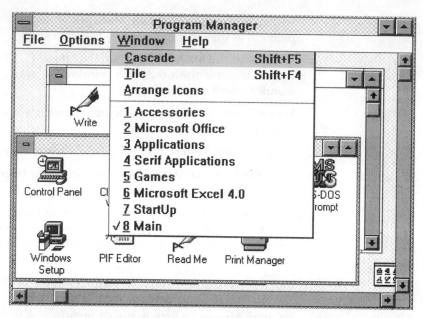

Figure 9

Move the screen pointer onto the menu option **Tile** and click.

The command is executed and the windows are arranged side by side on the desktop.

Open the **Window** menu again and this time choose the option **Cascade.**

This command displays the windows so that they overlap, keeping the window titles visible.

Now drag the three windows to new positions – place the screen pointer on the Title Bar of the window and drag.

Repeat the **Tile** command and the windows are re-arranged as before.

Finally select the **Cascade** option.

8. **Moving between windows.** Click anywhere on the **Main** window, then anywhere on the **Accessories** window. You will notice that clicking a window selects it so that it overlays the other ones and becomes the 'active' window. This is also confirmed by the title bar changing colour.

   Try this technique again for the **Program Manager** window. Unlike the other two windows it will not overlay other windows, but, as the controlling window it is always active – as confirmed by the colour of the Title Bar.

9. **Maximising and minimising windows.** Now we will experiment using the Maximise, Minimise and Restore buttons – see previous activity if necessary.

11

First maximise the **Program Manager** window – this presents no problem as the other two windows remain visible.

Now select the **Main** window and maximise it – in filling the whole screen it hides the other two windows – causing beginners to wonder where they have gone!

Simply open the **Window** menu again and select **Cascade** (or Tile). The three Windows re-appear.

Now click the **Restore** button on the Program Manager window.

Next click on the **Accessories** window – it becomes the active window.

Minimise the Accessories window – you may need to drag the minimise button into view. The window seems to disappear altogether; in fact it has become an icon on the Program Manager desktop.

Open the **Window** menu – you will see that only the Main option is ticked – indicating that this is the only window open (besides Program Manager which is always open)

Select the **Accessories** option from the menu and the window is opened again.
This is another way to open a window besides double clicking the icon on the Program Manager desktop. It is especially useful as a check on what windows are open, and as a way of opening Windows when their icons are hidden.

10. Closing Windows

The three windows that we are using are group windows – they contain further groups of icons rather than being applications in their own right. Minimising these windows closes them as we have just seen.

However we can also close a window using the Control-menu box in the top left hand corner of the window – see Figure 2 above. This can be useful if other parts of the window are hidden.

Activate the Main window. Click the Control-menu box on the **Main** window and a menu is opened – see Figure 10.

The top group of options duplicate ones we have already learnt.

Click the **Close** option and the active window is closed.

Now try the quicker method for the Accessories window – simply double click the Control-menu button and the window closes.
Only the Program Manager window should be open now.

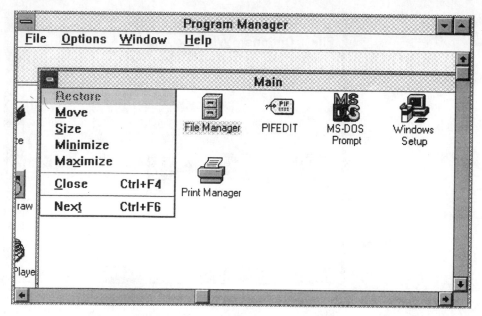

Figure 10

11. Re-arranging icons

You will have noticed that making windows smaller means that some of the icons disappear from view – Windows will not necessarily re-arrange them even if there is space available to do do. The reverse is also true to some extent – enlarging a window does not necessarily mean that all hidden icons will re-appear.

Open the **Options** menu and make sure that the **Auto Arrange** option is off, i.e. if it is ticked then click it to de-select the option.

When the Auto Arrange command on the Options menu is turned on (see above) then any icons that have been compressed together will spread out when a window is enlarged.

The commands on the Options menu are all examples of switch options – they can be set on or off by clicking them, *on* being indicated by a tick or check mark next to the option.

Now re-size the Program Manager window along the lines of Figure 11 so that only three of the icons are showing. (You can use the mouse to drag the icons around the desktop).

The presence of scroll bars tell you that there are icons currently not in view.

Open the **Window** menu and choose **Arrange Icons** – the icons are re-arranged on the desktop so that they can all be seen and the scroll bars disappear.

Now enlarge the desk top to normal size and choose the **Arrange Icons** option again. The icons should be arranged in their standard default layout along the bottom of the window.

13

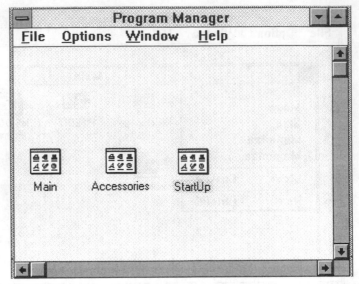

Figure 11

12. **Using Help.** Windows offers good help and tutorial facilities on basic operations, commands, concepts and technical information. You can call it up either by pressing the **F1** key or by using the Help option on the Menu Bar. Help can also be *context sensitive* – if you take a particular menu option or make an error you can get guidance tailored to what you are currently doing.

Open the Help menu; there are three main options:

Contents – lists topics alphabetically

Search for Help on – get help on a topic you specify

How to Use Help

Take this last option. A Help window appears – see Figure 12.

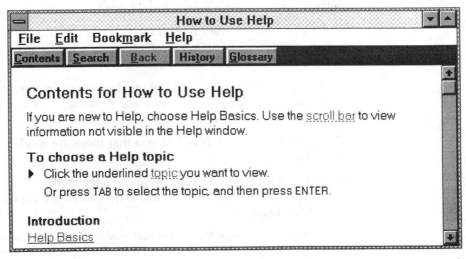

Figure 12

Notice that it shares many features with the Program Manager window – it has a Title Bar, Maximise and Minimise buttons, border for re-sizing, a scroll bar and a menu bar – though the menu options differ for this application.

Let's view the topics covered, we can take this opportunity to try out different scrolling techniques :

a. **Slow scrolling.** Position the screen pointer on the up or down arrow on the scroll bar and click once – the text scrolls a line at a time

b. **Continuous scrolling.** Position the screen pointer on the up or down arrow on the scroll bar and keep the mouse button pressed down – the text scrolls continuously

c. **Rapid scrolling.** Identify the square scroll box on the scroll bar – its position indicates your position in the document. Click above or below it and the help text moves up in window–sized blocks.

Try dragging this box now; you can move to the start or end of the document quickly

Choosing a Help topic. Scroll to the beginning of the Help window; you will notice that Help topics appear in a different colour to the rest of the text – usually green

Move the pointer onto the Introduction topic **'Help Basics'** – it becomes hand-shaped – and click – a new help window appears.

When you have read this window click the **Contents** button at the top of the screen – this will always return you to the table of contents

Now scroll down the Help window to the **'How to...'** section and select the topic, **Search for a Help Topic.** Read this help topic and then choose an option from this screen.

You are now on your third help screen and may want to return and review a previous help screen. Click the **Back** button at the top of the screen – you will be moved back one stage. Click it again and you are moved back a second stage.

Now click the **History** key at the top of the screen, this records the names of the Help windows you have already viewed. Double click on a topic and you will be returned to it (this is very useful prompt when you have forgotten the title of a Help screen)

Click the **Glossary** Button – it contains a list of Windows terms.

Scroll through the list and choose a few that interest you – a further window opens containing the meaning of the term.

Close the Glossary window using the Control-menu box – see section 10 above.

Now exit from Help using either the File menu or the Control-menu box.

13. **Dialogue boxes.** Open the Help menu again, this time choose the **Contents** option – you are taken into a Help Contents window , but this time it is context sensitive. The window is entitled Program Manager Help and offers a range of topics appropriate to the application from which it is called.

Now click the **Search** button; a window appears similar to Figure 13.

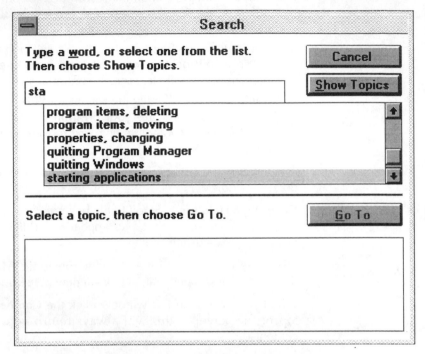

Figure 13

It includes an important Windows feature we have not come across yet – the dialogue box – a box which either contains a message or asks you to supply some information . Let's say that you want help on how to start an application. Begin typing the word **start** in the dialogue box as shown, and the list underneath will start scrolling to the relevant topic – **'Starting an Application'**

Click the **Show Topics** button next and the list box at the bottom of the window shows a list of topics; select one of these and then click the **Go To** button. A help screen appears on this topic.

When you have read it press the **Search** button and you are returned to the Search dialogue box.

This time instead of typing in the name of the topic, simply scroll through the list of topics and select one that interests you

Click the **Show Topics** button again, then the **Go To** button to call the Help Screen.

Now quit Help as before – see section 12 above.

16

Activity 4   Running the Windows tutorial

To review the fundamental skills that we have learnt in this unit we will run the Windows tutorial.

Simply open the **Help** menu and choose the option **Windows Tutorial.**

From then on it is fully interactive.

Summary of menu commands

Notes

Menu commands show the menu name first, followed by the command to choose from the menu, e.g. Edit-Clear means open the Edit menu and select the Clear command. Where a command is available from a particular window this is indicated in brackets.

Help – Contents	list topics alphabetically
Help – Search for Help on	find specified topic
Help – Windows Tutorial	Run Windows tutorial (Program Manager)
Window – Auto Arrange	Re-arrange icons automatically
Window – Arrange icons	Arrange icons in a window
Window – Tile	Display multiple windows side by side
Window – Cascade	Display multiple windows overlapping

unit 2
Creating and saving files

Introduction

In this unit you will be creating a set of files to use in later activities. You will be using two standard Windows applications, Notepad and Write, to do this. You will also learn how to save different versions of a file under different names and learn the rules for filenames.

Skills covered	Activity
Application – running	1, 8
Files – naming	1.10
Notepad – using	1
Saving	1.4, 1.7
Windows Write – using	2

Previous skills required	Covered in unit
Using the standard Windows components	1

Activity 1 Running an application from program manager

Note: You will need a suitable diskette (floppy disk) for this exercise, preferably a new one that does not contain any files.

A brand new disk needs to be formatted before it can be used – consult Unit 3, Activity 3 if necessary.

In this activity we will use Program Manager to run an application. An application is any program (or set of programs) that carries out a particular job, eg accounts, or word processor. The standard Program Manager window is a *group window,* it normally contains no applications; instead it contains icons such as Main, Accessories, Applications etc which, when opened, lead to further groups of applications.

We are going to use Notepad as our example application which is normally located on the Accessories desktop. It is a text editor, (rather like a very simple word processor) We will use it to create some short text files, but as we will see later it has other uses too.

18

1. Make sure that the **Accessories** desk top is open.

   Find the icon labelled **Notepad** and double click it.

   The hour glass icon confirms that the application is loading (ie Windows looks for the application program on the hard disk and loads it into the computer's main memory)

2. A blank notepad window is displayed, waiting for you to enter some text – see Figure 1.

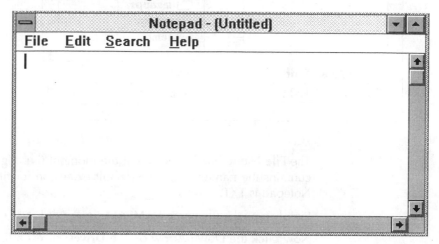

Figure 1

   Notice that it contains many standard windows features that you have already used, eg title, menu and scroll bars as well as maximise and minimise buttons.

   The flashing bar indicates the insertion point for the text.

3. **Creating text files.** For your future activities in Windows and MS-DOS you will need a set of files for you to work with. These can be 'dummy' files, meaning that it doesn't really matter what they contain as you will be using them to practise such operations as listing, copying, renaming and sorting. So if your typing skills are minimal merely fill them with a jumble of characters. (lecturers using these units as a course text can obtain these files on disk from the publishers – see preface)

   First open the **Edit** menu and select the **Word Wrap** option. This ensures that the when the text that you type reaches the end of the line it 'wraps round' to the next line.

   Simply type in a few lines of text now.

4. **Saving files.** At the moment the text that you have created is only saved in the computer's main memory. It has the temporary name 'Untitled' and will be lost as soon as you exit the notebook application unless you save it as a named file.

   Open the **File** menu and choose the **Save As** option. The Save As dialogue box appears next – see Figure 2.

19

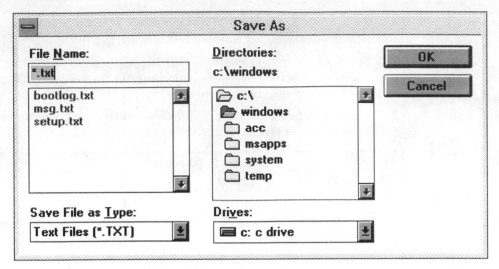

Figure 2

The **File Name** box is selected at the moment (i.e. highlighted) and contains the name *.TXT. The default extension for files created in Notepad is TXT.

Simply type the file name **MEMSAL1** (upper or lower case).

Now click the Down Arrow on the **Drives:** box – a list of available drives appears – see Figure 3.

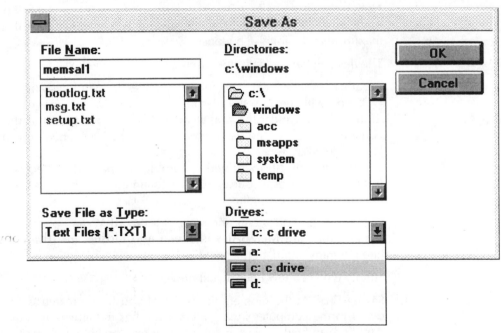

Figure 3

In the activities in these units we shall be using a diskette to save work. **A**: is your diskette drive; make sure that you have a suitable formatted diskette in A drive.

If you are using a brand new diskette it may need formatting – see Unit 3, Activity 3.

Now choose the **A** drive – the Drives box displays this information.

Finally click the **OK** box. The command is executed and the file MEMSAL1 is saved to diskette, the drive light comes on to show that the Notepad data is being written (saved) to disk.

A note on drives. On your PC drive C, the hard disk, is used to store Windows and MS-DOS and often other applications, e.g. word processor, spreadsheet or database. If you have enough disk space you can also use C or another hard disk to save work that you create. However it is common to save work on a diskette (also known as a floppy disk) especially where space on the hard disk is limited or if you want to work on more than one computer.

5. The dialogue box disappears and you are returned to the Notepad window which now displays the file name of the newly saved file MEMSAL1.TXT (see the 'Notes on File Names' section at the end of this Activity)

6. **Saving changes.** Add a few more lines of text to this file. These changes will need saving permanently to disk too.

    Open the File menu; this time choose the **Save** option. (*not Save as*)

    The drive light comes on again indicating that the changes are being permanently saved to to the MEMSAL1 file on disk.

7. **Saving a file under a new name.** Add a few more lines of text to the file; Open the **File** menu again, but this time choose the **Save As** option.

    The Save As dialogue box appears; amend the file name to **MEMSAL2.TXT**

    Make sure that the Drives: box still shows **A:**

    Click the **OK** button.

    The drive light comes on as before to show that the new file MEMSAL2.TXT is being written (saved) to disk.

8. The Notepad window now displays the file name MEMSAL2.TXT - the original file MEMSAL1 is saved and closed and the copy opened.

    Now we'll use this method again to create six more files; first add a few more lines of text (this means that all files will vary slightly in size), then choose Save As from the File menu as before.

Name the files that you create as follows :

MEMSAL3.TXT

MEMSAL4.TXT

MEMACC1.TXT

MEMACC2.TXT

MEMACC3.TXT

MEMACC4.TXT

When you have created these files open the **File** menu and select the **Open** option; your display should resemble Figure 4.

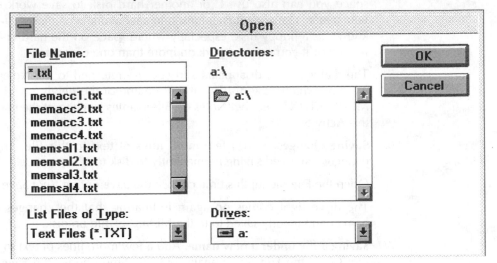

Figure 4

ie 8 text files have been created using the Notepad application.

Click the **Cancel** button on the Open dialogue box.

9. **Note on naming conventions.** The file naming convention used reserves the first three letters for the type of document; MEM = memo.

Letters 4 – 6 are reserved for the department, ACC = Accounts and SAL = Sales.

The final number on the file name is the order of creation and ensures that each file name is unique.

The filename is separated by a full stop from the 3 letter extension TXT
The extension is optional for most types of files, (see note on file names at the end of this activity) The Notepad application automatically assigns the extension .TXT to documents created in it.

When you are creating files make sure that you use a meaningful, memorable naming convention and stick to it.

10. **Exiting and Saving a File.** Add another line to the final file that you have created. Now try to exit the Notepad application as follows; open the **File** menu and select **Exit.** A dialogue box appears, reminding you that you have not saved the changes made to the document – see Figure 5.

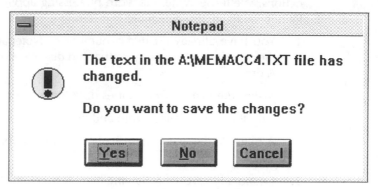

Figure 5

All Windows applications have this feature reminding you to save your work. Normally you would click the Yes button which saves and exits the document.

Click the **Cancel** button which returns you to the document. A situation where you *would* find it useful to click the No button and exit a document without saving is if you have made some major unwanted change to a document e.g. a deletion. Exiting without saving would leave the document as it was the last time it was saved, before you made the alteration – although you would also also lose any other changes that you had made.

Now exit the Notepad application again this time selecting the Yes option on the Dialogue box.

Notes on filenames

In MS-DOS and Windows a file name can consist of up to 8 characters, these can be the letters A to Z (upper or lower case) or numbers 0 to 9.

Certain other keyboard characters can be used, including the dash (-),

The underscore character (_), can also be used.

The following **cannot** be used: space, comma, full stop, slash, colon, semicolon, brackets and quotation marks and the equals sign.

The filename is usually followed by an extension of up to three characters, separated from the filename by a full stop or 'dot'.

The extension usually identifies the type of file, and is often automatically allocated by the program which creates it.

Activity 2 Independent activities

You have now run an application – Notepad – and used it to create some simple text files. Let's experiment with running some other applications. We'll use Write, the word processing application supplied with Windows, to create some more text files.

1. You have already created a number of Notepad documents – see the previous activity; ensure that the diskette storing these files is in A drive.

    Make sure that the Accessories desk top is open as before

    Find the icon labelled Write and double click it.

    A blank Write window is displayed, waiting for you to enter some text.

2. Create and save the following eight dummy files onto A drive in the same way as you did in the Notebook application in the previous activity.

    LETSAL1.JM

    LETSAL2.WRI

    LETSAL3.WRI

    LETSAL4.WRI

    LETTACC1.WRI

    LETACC2.WRI

    LETACC3.WRI

    LETACC4.WRI

    Notice that **.WRI** is the default extension for files created in Write. This distinguishes from them from other files such as Notebook files which have the extension .TXT. However you are free to use no extension at all or any other extension such as .JM

    Up to three letters or numbers may be used – see the previous activity for rules on file names and extensions. As we will see in later units, not using the default extension causes complications; it means that selecting the file will not automatically start the application.

3. When you have created all the above files quit the Windows Write application – this time do so by clicking the Control menu box at the top left corner of the Write Window – see Figure 6.

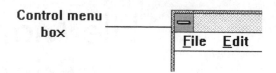

Control menu box

Figure 6

Note Be careful to identify the correct Control-menu box, if there are two in view, one or the Program Manager desktop and one for the Write application as in the above diagram, take the one for the Write application.

Select the Close option on the Control-menu.

The Write application is closed and you are returned to the Program Manager desktop.

Summary of menu commands

Notes

Menu commands show the menu name first, followed by the command to choose from the menu, e.g. Edit-Clear means open the Edit menu and select the Clear command. Where a command is available from a particular window this is indicated in brackets.

File – Exit	Exit from an application
File – Open	Open an existing file
File – Print	Print contents of a file
File – Save	Save changes to an existing file
File – Save as	Name and save a new file/copy a file and rename it

25

unit 3

File Manager and Print Manager

Introduction

In this unit you will be learning more about File Manager – how to view files held on disk and sort them into different orders. You will also be finding out how to format a disk and make a copy of it. Finally you will learn how to exit Windows

Skills covered	Activity
Disk drive – selecting	1.2
Diskette – copying	4
Diskette – formatting	3
File Manager – using	1,2
Files – opening	5
Files – sorting	1.3
Printing	6
Windows – exiting	7
Windows Write – using	6

Previous skills required	Covered in unit
Using the standard Windows components	1

Resources required

Practice files created in Unit 2

Activity 1   File Manager – keeping track of your files

This activity gives you a brief tour of File Manager. The more advanced features are covered in Unit 5.

1. File Manager is part of the Main group. If the Main desktop has been shrunk to an icon then Double-click it and the Main desktop is opened – see Figure 7 in Unit 1 if necessary.

   Now double click the File Manager icon and the window shown in Figure 1 appears.

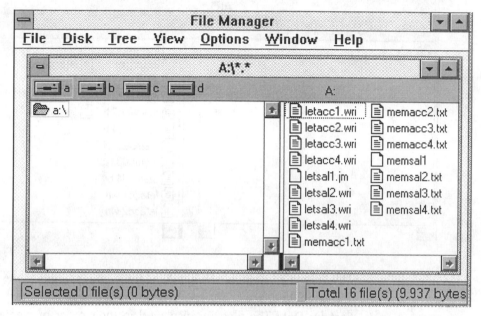

Figure 1

It contains the now familiar Windows features – title, menu and scroll bars, plus Maximise and Minimise buttons.

On the desk top are icons representing files, directories and disk drives. Your window may be different to this.

File Manager allows you to change from one disk drive to another and view the files that you have. It also allows you to copy, move and delete files, skills that we will be learning in Units 6 and 7.

2. **Selecting a disk drive.** Look at the disk icons displayed underneath the title bar. The icon for the A drive should be outlined – see Figure 1 above.

   If not click the A drive icon.

   The files that we have just created on diskette should be displayed on the right side of the window. Check that all 16 files are present – if not return to the previous unit and complete them.

   Look at the Title of the desktop – **A:*.*** This tells you that the disk currently in use is A, the floppy or diskette drive.

3. Using the View menu at the top of the screen, we can view the files in a variety of ways.

   Open the **View** menu and try these **Sort by** options:

27

Sort by Name is the default option – the files on disk are in alphabetic order of file name.

Sort by Type – the files are sorted into order of their extension – see Figure 2.

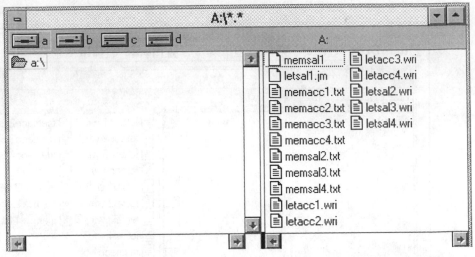

Figure 2

This allows us to group all the .WRI files together, all the .TXT files and so on.

Sort by Date The files are displayed in their order of creation; to see the dates select the 'All File Details options' from the View menu.

This also shows the file size in bytes.

4. **Independent activity.**

   Identify the following files on your diskette:

   The largest file.

   The file created last – look at the time as well as the date.

   How many files do not use the .TXT or .WRI extension?

5. Open the **View** menu again and select the **Name** option.

   Open the **View** menu and select **Sort by Name** – the default display.

Activity 2 Using File Manager to start an application

As you have seen, File Manager provides a quick and easy way of finding files on disk; once you have located a file you can open it directly from File Manager.

1. Find the file MEMSAL2.TXT that you created in the Notepad application and double click the icon.

   The file will be opened, overlaying the File Manager Window – there was no need to open the Notepad application and then the file. File Manager performs these operations for you.

2. Close the MEMSAL1 file – open the **File** menu and choose the **Exit** option.

   You are returned to the File Manager window. As the file was not changed you were not prompted to save it.

   Exit from File Manager too but use this alternative method:

   Double click on the Control-menu box at the top right of the File Manager screen.

   (if there are two as in Figure 3 then take the top one)

click the top Control-menu box

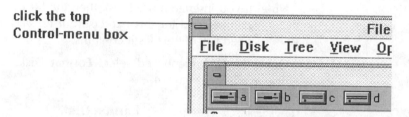

Figure 3

Activity 3 Formatting a diskette

Introduction

A new diskette it is normally sold unformatted; it cannot be used until it has been formatted. To practise this activity you will need another diskette, preferably new and unused. I am assuming that your PC takes the standard three and a half inch, high density 1.44 Mb diskettes.

Formatting or initialising divides the diskette into electro-magnetic tracks so that information can be stored on it. If you format a used disk then any information already stored on it will erased. It cannot be restored using Windows but the MS-DOS Unformat command can restore the information .

Recognising high density disks. All new PC's use the standard three and a half inch, high density 1.44 Mb diskettes. However the older double density 720Kb disks can be read by the newer high density drives.

How many square holes does your disk have? All disks have one – the write protect notch which can be opened to protect the files from being changed.

Only high density disks have a second hole – this is your best guide, though some manufacturers stamp 'HD' on their disks.

1. Start Windows if necessary and make sure that File Manager is open.

    Insert a new, *unused* diskette in A drive.

    The files from the previous diskette used may still be displayed. Open the **Window** menu and select **Refresh.** File Manager searches the new disk for files.

    If you have inserted a new, unformatted disk it will be unreadable and you will receive the message:

    'The disk in drive A is not formatted. Do you want to format it now?'

    Click the **No** button.

    Note: If you inserted a used disk then the files will be displayed, it can be used for this exercise but check that you no longer need any of the files it contains.

2. Open the **Disk** menu and select **Format Disk.** A dialogue box is displayed – see Figure 4.

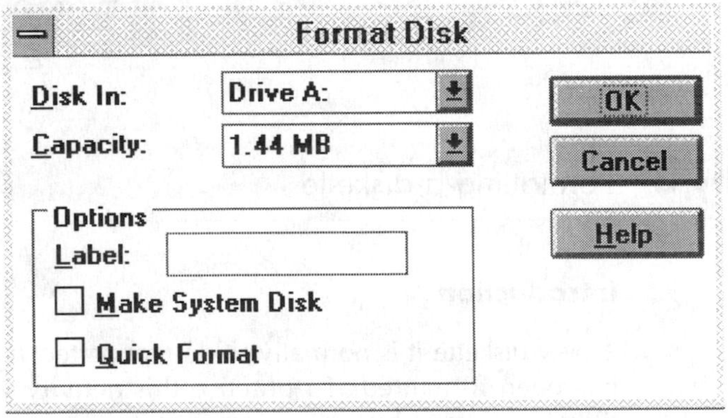

Figure 4

The first two options are already selected :

Drive A: Normally you will only have this one diskette drive. If not click the down arrow button and select the drive letter that you want to use.

Capacity: All modern Pc's use 1.44Mb disks – see introduction. If you are using a double density disk then click the down arrow box and select 720K.

Complete the other options as follows:

Label: Allows you to give the disk a volume label. This is displayed in File Manager whenever the drive icon is selected. It is a useful identifier and can be up to 11 characters.

Click this box and enter a suitable label eg **backup-files.**

30

Make System Disk: We will be finding out more about system disks in a later activity. Leave this box unchecked.

Quick Format: Click the **Help** button to find out more about this; remember to exit from Help afterwards.

If you are using a disk that has *already* been formatted you can click this box. It is now checked – a cross appears in it.

Finally click the **OK** button. A message appears, warning you that any data on the disk will be erased. If it is a new disk there is no data to erase; if you not using a new disk you must be sure that there is no vital data on this diskette.

If you are happy then click the **Yes** button.

A formatting disk message appears while the formatting takes place – if you are not using Quick Format then this is a fairly slow process.

3. Eventually this is replaced by the following dialogue box – see Figure 5.

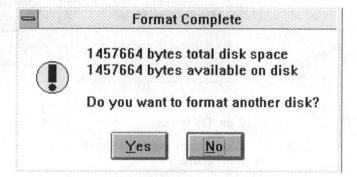

Figure 5

It reports that your diskette now has a storage capacity of 1.44 plus megabytes. ie it holds approximately 1.44 million characters or bytes.

Click the **No** button and return to File Manager.

Activity 4 Copying a disk

Introduction

Now that we have formatted a diskette we are going to use it to take a backup copy of the dummy practise files that we have created. Although modern computer media are very reliable there is always the danger that your diskette may be lost, stolen or damaged. It is foolhardy not to back up important data regularly. Diskettes may be cheap to replace, but the data they contain certainly is not!

1. Remove the diskette that you have just formatted from the drive and make sure that it has a label. Write on it the following:

    your name and point of contact, e.g. 'J SMITH B Sc 1 Computing'

    The disks contents, e.g. 'Backup Windows Dummy Files'.

    Make sure that the label is updated when required.

2. Suitably label the original diskette containing the 16 dummy files and insert it in A drive.

    Open the **Window** menu and select **Refresh.** Check that the dummy files are on the disk.

3. Open the **Disk** menu and select **Copy Disk.**

4. A dialogue box appears – see Figure 6.

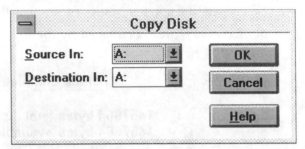

Figure 6

    Click the **OK** button.

5. A dialogue box warns you that all data will be erased from the destination disk.

    Click the Yes button.

    A third dialogue box asks you to ' Insert source disk'. The source disk is already inserted – click the OK button.

6. A 'Copying Disk' message appears next. The files are being copied from *source* disk into main memory. This is a fairly slow process which records the progress of the copying. Eventually a further message is displayed telling you to insert the *destination* disk – where the files are to be copied to.

7. Remove the source disk and insert the destination disk, i.e. the disk that you have just formatted and labelled.

    Click the **OK** button.

    The 'Copying Disk' message appears again. When it is 100% complete the message disappears.

    File Manager shows the copied files on the desk top – see Figure 1 above.

    Note: With disks containing more data you may need to swap the source and destination disks over more than once.

8. Remove the backup disk from A drive. As an additional safeguard open the write-protect hole on the disk. This will prevent the files being amended or deleted.

   You will need to close it again whenever you wish to modify the contents of the disk.

9. Insert the original source diskette in A drive.

Activity 5 Opening a file from within an application

Introduction

We've just seen that File Manager allows you to keep track of all the files on your disks. However, if you are already using an application such as Notebook or Write you don't need to exit to File Manager. It's just as easy to find and retrieve a file when you are working in an application.

In this activity we'll be using Windows Write as an example but the steps are essentially the same for all Windows applications – spreadsheets, databases, word processors or whatever.

1. Open the **Accessories** desktop and open the **Write** Application.

   A blank Write document appears with the default title 'Untitled'

   You have already created a number of Write documents in Unit 2; ensure that the diskette storing these files is in A drive.

2. Open the **File** menu and select the **Open** option.

   The Open dialogue box appears – see Figure 7.

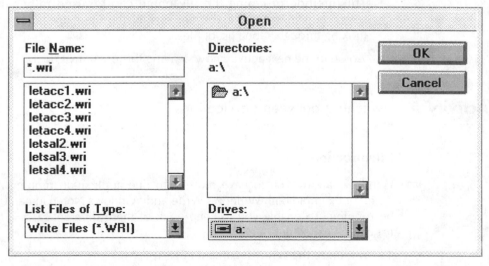

Figure 7

Look at the **Drives** box – is A currently the active drive?

33

If not click the down arrow button attached to the Drives box. A list box opens.

Click A drive icon to select it.

The Directories box should now be headed a:\ This confirms that you have changed to A drive.

The File Name box shows seven files ending with the standard WRI extension as you are opening a file from the Write application WRI. Any other files on disk with different extensions, eg .TXT are not listed.

3. Select the file **LETSAL2.WRI** then click the **OK** button.

Windows looks for this file on your Diskette (notice that the drive light on the front of the PC lights up)

The Write window appears with the text of the LETSAL2.WRI

You now know how to retrieve a file from within an application. Let's try this once more, this time for the document LETACC4.WRI

Repeat the above steps. The previous document LETSAL2.WRI is closed and the document LETACC4.WRI replaces it in the Write window.

4. A file can also be retrieved by typing the name (and extension if any) in the File Name box.

To retrieve the document LETSAL1.JM open the **File** menu and select the **Open** option as before.

Now when the Open dialogue box appears – see Figure 7 above – simply type the file name LETSAL1.JM in the File Name box and click OK.

This method of typing the file name can be used rather than selecting it from a list if you are sure of the file name – it avoids looking through a long list of files.

5. Go on to the next activity now, leaving this document open.

Activity 6   Switching between applications

Introduction

Windows allows you to have more than one application running at a time, for example both Windows Write and Windows Notepad can both be running. To enable you to keep track of these different tasks a task list can be called up.

1. Minimise the Write document LETSAL1.JM.

Open the **Accessories** desktop and open the **Notepad** application.

A blank document appears with the default title 'Untitled'.

2. Hold down the **Ctrl** key then press the **Esc** key.

   A task list opens showing three tasks currently running – the third one is Program Manager (which is of course always running)

   Click on the **Write** task then click the **Switch to** button – it becomes the active application.

3. Press the Ctrl-Esc keys again and activate the other tasks

   Notice also that the **Cascade** and **Tile** options are available – see Unit 1.

4. Now Hold down the **Alt** key and press the **Tab** key – this key combination can also be used to cycle through the tasks that are running. Try this and return to the Write document.

5. Finally press the Ctrl-Esc keys again and select the **Notepad** application.

   Click the **End Task** button – the Notepad application is closed.

   Open the Write document again if necessary.

   Note: Use the task list to check on which tasks are running, close unnecessary tasks and to switch between tasks.

Activity 7 Printing a document

Introduction

If you have created something in a Windows application all that you normally need to do is to open the File menu and select the Print option. You can then specify the number of copies and other details. In the background controlling printing is the Windows *Print Manager,* which the user is normally unaware of. The main uses of Print Manager are to set up the printer, change the printer settings, or to check on the status of a print job.

1. In this activity we will be printing off the Write document LETSAL1.JM. If this document is not open then repeat the previous activity

2. **The Printer.** Check that the printer is:

   Switched on.

   Set online – check switch and warning light.

   Connected via cable to your computer.

   Has paper in it.

   Note: If you have no functioning printer you can still carry out the following steps, but an error message will appear if you attempt to print

35

3. Open the **File** menu and select **Print.**

The Print window appears next, showing a dialogue box where you can make your selection – see Figure 8.

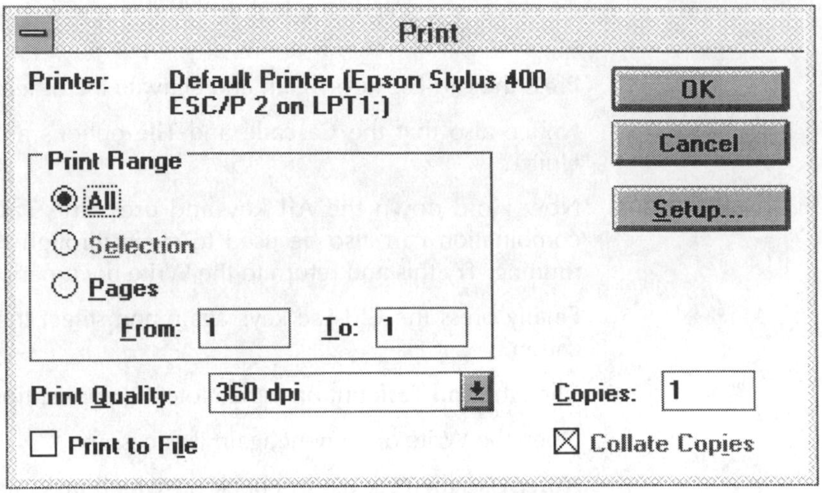

Figure 8

If you are connected to a printer then click the **OK** button.

A 'Now Printing' message appears on screen and the document starts to print.

If you are not connected to a printer press the **Cancel** button

4. Finally use the File menu to exit from Write, you are returned to the Windows desktop.

Activity 8   Exiting Windows

Exiting Program Manager will end your Windows session.

There are several ways of doing this:

a.   Double-click the Control-menu box on the File Manager window.

b.   Open the Control-menu on the File Manager window and choose the Close option.

c.   Open the File menu on the File Manager window and choose the Exit Windows option.

Whichever method you use a dialogue box will appear asking you to confirm.

In which case click the **OK** button to exit or the **Cancel** button to resume Windows.

If you have been using an application and have omitted to save some work then another dialogue box will prompt you to save it.

Summary of menu commands

Notes

Menu commands show the menu name first, followed by the command to choose from the menu, e.g. Edit-Clear means open the Edit menu and select the Clear command. Where a command is available from a particular window this is indicated in brackets.

Alt –Tab	Switch between tasks.
Ctrl – Esc	Call up task list
File – Exit	Exit from an application/Windows
File – Print (File Manager)	Print contents of a file
Disk – Copy Disk	Make copy of diskette Disk – Format Format a disk
View – Sort by...	View list of files in various orders – name, date etc
Window – Refresh	Updates Window display

37

Program Manager – organising your applications

Introduction

We have already used Program Manager in Unit 1. It is the central point from which all other Windows applications begin, and usually the first window that you see when you start up Windows. – see Figure 1.

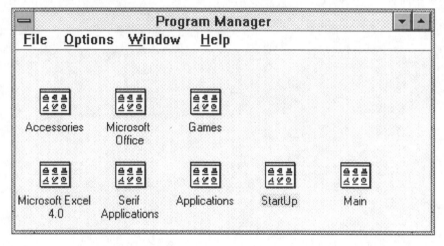

Figure 1

Closing Program Manager ends your Windows session.

Group windows and applications

Program Manager has two main purposes – to start applications and to organise them into convenient groups.

You will recall that an application is any program (or set of programs) that carries out a particular job. To start one is simply a matter of double clicking it. (In Unit 2 for example we used the Notepad and the Write applications to produce some small text files) Program Manager is a *group window;* it contains no applications itself, it contains further groups of applications – Main, Accessories, Applications etc. When not being used these group windows are normally shrunk to icons in the Program Manager window – See Figure 1 above. When a group window is opened the set of icons for the different applications is displayed – see Figure 2.

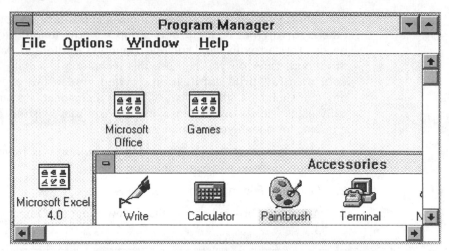

Figure 2

The icons representing applications are called *program-item* icons. However you don't need to stick rigidly to these initial groupings, Program Manager allows you to:

Create new groups of applications to suit your own needs

Move or copy applications from one group to another

Remove items from a group

Start applications automatically when Windows is started

You will find that tailoring Windows to your own ways of working is easy and can make you more productive.

Skills covered	**Activity**
Formula bar – displaying	2.8
Group items – adding and deleting	3
Group windows – creating	1
Group windows – deleting and restoring	7
INI files – viewing	5
Settings – saving	2
Startup applications – creating	4

Previous skills required	**Covered in unit**
Using the standard Windows components	1

Activity 1   Creating a new group

You'll find yourself using some Windows applications a lot more than others, so why not create a new group window tailored to your own needs? To start with we'll include Windows Write and Paintbrush in this group. Later on you can use this technique to create a group for your own favourite applications. When you install a commercial program such as a spreadsheet or word processor it is often automatically placed in its own group window. You may wish to change this grouping for one of your own.

1. Make sure that the Program Manager window is open. Close all other windows to avoid confusion.

2. Open the **File** menu and select **New.**

3. A dialogue box appears entitled New Program Object – see Figure 3.

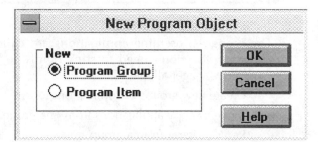

Figure 3

Make sure that the button labelled **Program Group** is selected – a dot appears in it when selected.

Click the **OK** button.

4. Another dialogue box appears entitled Program Group Properties.

Enter the name **Toolbar** as shown in Figure 4 (leave the Group File box blank)

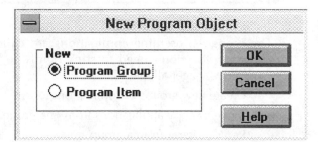

Figure 4

Click the **OK** button.

5. The new empty group window entitled Toolbar appears. We can now move applications into it.
    Make sure that the Accessories group window is open and that the Write and Paintbrush applications are visible – see Figure 5.

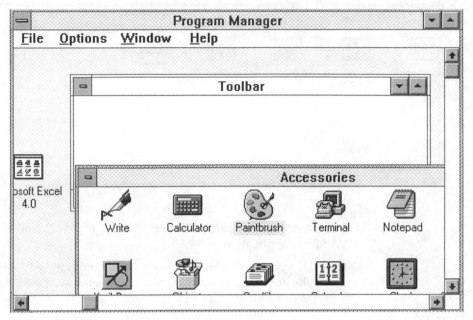

Figure 5

6. Hold down the **Ctrl** key and drag the Write icon from the Accessories window to the Toolbar window. The screen pointer becomes a copy of the application that you are copying.

7. Repeat this operation for the Paintbrush icon.

8. **Notes:** The Paintbrush and Write icons have been copied – the originals are still in the Accessories Window. However there is still only one copy of the program on the disk – we have merely made it accessible from two windows by copying the icon.
    If you want to *move* an icon rather than copy it then don't hold down the Ctrl key when you are dragging the icon.

9. Now close all the group windows except for Toolbar and Program Manager.

    Re-size the Toolbar window so that it resembles Figure 6.

41

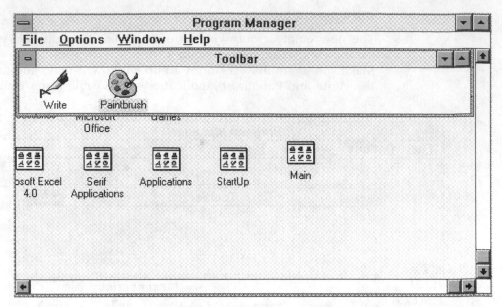

Figure 6

You have now created a similar toolbar to ones used in many Windows applications.

Hints: If you are working on your own computer you can copy the icons from major applications such as Excel, Lotus or Word so that you can start them from your toolbar window.

If you wish to rename an icon then proceed as follows :

Click on the icon – the colour changes

Open the File menu and select the Properties option

A dialogue box appears – amend the name in the Description box.

Click OK. The icon is re-named

10. Now carry out the next activity before exiting Windows.

Activity 2   Saving windows settings

You can save the windows settings created in the last activity so that your personal toolbar is displayed whenever you start Windows.

1. Open the **Options** menu and select **Save Settings on Exit** – it is now ticked.

2. Now exit Windows in the usual way.

3. Start Windows again – the settings are saved from the previous session.

42

Hint: Once you have arranged the Windows to your liking it is a good idea to open the Options menu again and de-select the Save Settings on Exit option. In this way you can ensure that any changes made during Windows operations will **not** be saved when you use Windows again.

Activity 3   Deleting and adding group items

From time to time you may want to remove applications from a group window and add new ones. Let's say that you want to remove the Write application and add the Notebook.

1. Make sure that the Toolbar group window is open – see Figure 6 above.

2. Click the **Write** icon in the Toolbar window once to select it.

3. Open the **File** menu and select **Delete** – a confirmation message appears.

4. Click the **Yes** button and the Write icon is deleted. (only the icon representing the application has been deleted, the Write program is still on disk and can be run from the Accessories window or File Manager as usual)

5. Now open the **Accessories** window and ensure that the Notepad icon is in view.

6. Hold down the **Ctrl** Key and and drag the Notepad icon from the Accessories window to the Toolbar Window.

7. The Toolbar Window should now resemble Figure 7 and contain the Paintbrush and the Notepad icons.

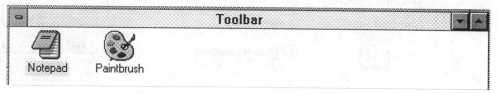

Figure 7

Activity 4   Creating startup applications

There may be an application that you tend to use first when you start Windows, this might be a word processor or spreadsheet, or a Windows utility such as Clock or Calendar. Program Manager provides a Startup Group for this purpose.

Any application placed in a startup group will be automatically started and ready for use whenever you start Windows. They can be either fully running in their own windows, or displayed as icons, ready to be

43

opened. However you should restrict startup applications to those that you will definitely need when you start Windows; it takes time to load up individual applications and therefore any startup application will prolong the time Windows takes to load.

1. Make sure that the **Accessories** and the **Startup** group windows are both open.

2. Hold down the **Ctrl** key and drag the Clock and the Calendar applications from the Accessories window to the Startup window.

3. Open the **Options** menu and make sure that **Save Settings on Exit** is selected. (ticked)

4. Now exit and restart Windows. The Clock application opens automatically, followed quickly by the Calendar.

5. Let's organise the startup group so that calendar is displayed as an icon rather than in its own window.
   Close both of these icons using the File menu or the Control-menu box. They are reduced to icons in the Startup window.

6. Click the Calendar icon **once** to select it.

7. Open the **File** menu of Program Manager and select **Properties.**

   A dialogue box appears – see Figure 8.

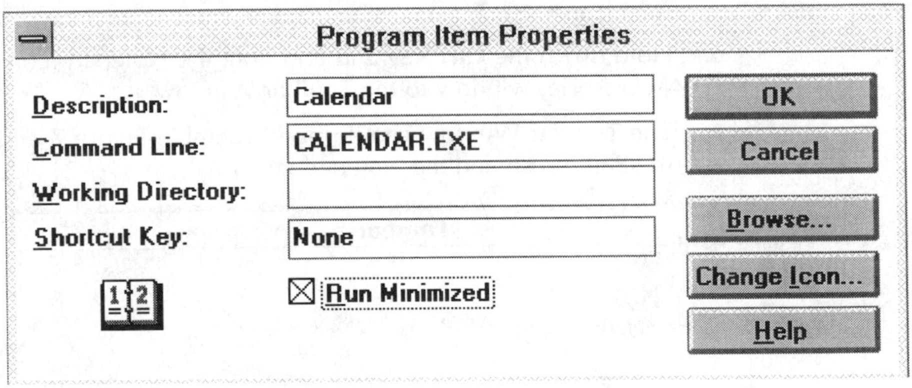

Program Item Properties		
Description:	Calendar	OK
Command Line:	CALENDAR.EXE	Cancel
Working Directory:		
Shortcut Key:	None	Browse...
	☒ Run Minimized	Change Icon...
		Help

Figure 8

Click the **Run Minimised** box – an X appears in it.

Click the **OK** button

8. Now double click the clock icon – the window opens. Re-size it and drag it to the top of the screen so that it resembles Figure 9.

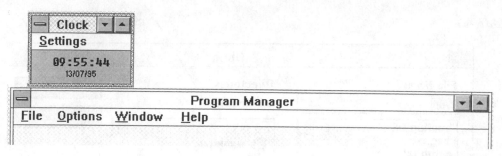

Figure 9

9. Now exit and restart Windows. The Clock application starts in a convenient location at the top of the screen. The Run Minimised command ensures that the calendar application starts as an icon, thereby saving the time taken to load the program. This is a useful technique if you have several startup applications. If you use a Startup window you should try limiting the startup applications to one main application, and set others to run minimised.

Activity 5   Behind the scenes – .INI Files

You have created two new group windows, the **Toolbar** window to hold applications that you use most often, and a **Startup** window that runs applications automatically when Windows starts. The various group windows are controlled by a file called PROGMAN.INI that records the various settings for File Manager. It is one of a large group of .INI files that set up (**INI**tialise) the way Windows works. Although they can be modified using a text editor such as Notepad or the MS-DOS editor, these units do not teach these skills nor do they encourage beginners to experiment on their own! Doing so can degrade the performance of Windows or even stop it running altogether and is especially irresponsible if others have to use a PC as well as you. However we can have a look at how two of them are set up.

1. Open the Notepad application – use either the Toolbar window or the Accessories window.

2. Open the **File** menu on the Notepad window and select the **Open** option.

   The Open dialogue Box appears – see Figure 10.

   First check the Directories heading at the top of the screen. If it reads **c:\windows** then skip the next two sections and go on to section 5.

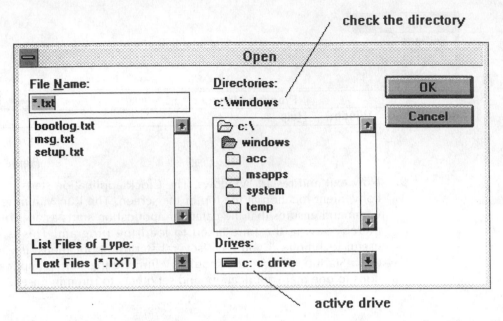

Figure 10

3. Look at the **Drives** box at the bottom of the window – is C currently the active drive?
    If not click the down arrow button attached to the Drives box.

    A list box opens.

    Click the C drive icon to select it.

    The Directories box should now be headed **C:**

    This confirms that you have changed to C drive.

4. Now we need to make sure that we are in the Windows directory (a directory is a section of the disk that holds related files – see unit 6 for a more detailed explanation)

    Look in the list box underneath the Directories heading – see Figure 10 above – can you see the Windows directory? If not you may need to scroll it into view.

    Double click on the Windows icon – the Windows directory is now opened and the Directories box is now headed **c:\windows**

5. **The PROGMAN.INI File.** As you are opening a file from the Notepad application the File Name box only shows the files in the Windows directory ending with the extension .TXT . This is the default extension given to all file created in Notepad and no other types of file are listed.

    Type the file name PROGMAN.INI then click the **OK** button.

    Windows looks for this file in the Windows directory and the Notepad window appears with the text of the PROGMAN.INI.

The Groups section –see example below – shows which group windows have been set up as files with the special Extension .GRP

You may have a slightly different set, but you will probably have the standard ones – Main, Accessories, Startup and Applications groups, plus the special Toolbar group that we have created,

[Groups]

Group1=C:\WINDOWS\MAIN.GRP

Group2=C:\WINDOWS\ACCESSOR.GRP

Group3=C:\WINDOWS\GAMES.GRP

Group4=C:\WINDOWS\STARTUP.GRP

Group5=C:\WINDOWS\APPLICAT.GRP

Group6=C:\WINDOWS\TOOLBAR.GRP

6.   **The WIN.INI File.** Use Notepad to display the WIN.INI file. It is a lengthy file used by Program Manager to hold details of how Windows is set up on your PC. Amendments are usually made via the Control Panel rather than editing the file directly. It is divided into sections each of which has a heading in square brackets. It is only possible to explain them here in very general terms. Identify the following sections in your WIN.INI file:

Windows section – controls eg cursor blink rate, mouse click and keyboard speed

Desktop and colors sections – control the colour and appearance of Windows components

Fonts section – lists the Fonts available to Windows.

Which section do you think control the currency symbol and date conventions?

7.   Exit from Notepad *without making any changes* and return to Program Manager.

Activity 6   Re-naming and deleting a group window

You already know how to create group windows and how to add and remove applications. In this activity you will learn how to change the name of a group window and how to delete the entire window when you no longer need it. We will practise these operations on the Toolbar window that we have created.

1.   Make sure that all windows except Program Manager are minimised.

Click the Toolbar icon once to select it – don't worry if a menu opens – see Figure 11.

47

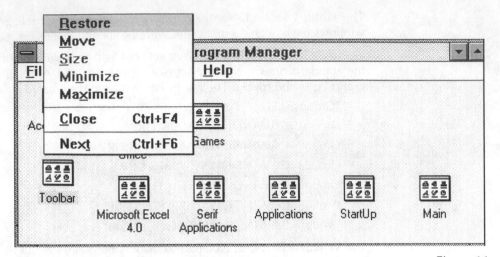

Figure 11

2. Open the **File** menu and select **Properties** – a dialogue box opens.

   Amend the description to 'Personal Toolbar' – see Figure 12.

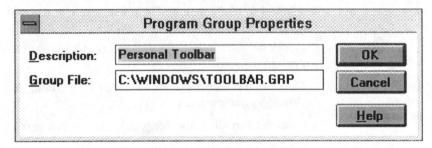

Figure 12

   Click **OK** and the group window is renamed.

3. To delete the entire group window and the applications that it contains first repeat step 1 above.

4. Open the **File** menu and select **Delete** – a dialogue box opens.

   Click Yes and the group window is deleted.

Troubleshooting – Restoring a deleted group window. (Information only)

   If you have accidentally deleted one of the pre-defined group windows such as Games or Accessories don't worry – it can be easily restored by one of the following methods;

Method 1 Restoring Accessories and Games groups

1. Open the Main group window and double click the Windows Setup icon. A dialogue box appears.

2. Open the Options menu on the dialogue box and choose Add/Remove Windows Components.

   A second Setup dialogue box opens, that lists various optional components of Windows, including the Accessories and Games groups – see Figure 13

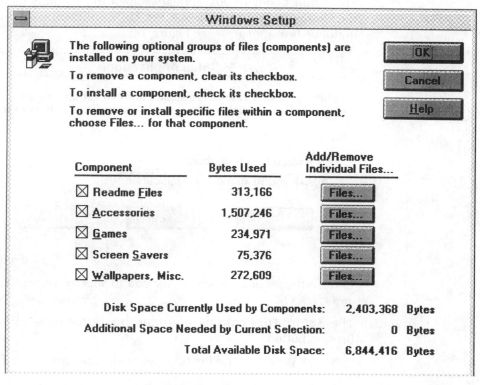

Figure 13

3. If a component is not checked, i.e. no 'X' appears in the check box then it has been removed.

   If you wish to restore it click the appropriate box – a dialogue box appears, asking you to insert the appropriate Windows disk.

   Insert the disk in the drive and click OK

Method 2 Restoring Main and Applications group windows

If you have accidentally the Main or Applications groups don't panic! The program items have not been removed from hard disk, only their icons and the group window containing them have been removed.

First use the skills that you have learnt to re-create the group window that you have deleted – see Activity 1 above.

1. Open the Main group window and double click the Setup icon.

   If you have removed the Main group Window then you will have to run Setup from Program Manager

49

Open the File menu on the Program Manager group window and select Run.

The Run dialogue box appears

Enter the program name SETUP and click OK.

2. The Setup dialogue box appears. Open the Options menu on the dialogue box and choose Set Up Applications. A further dialogue box appears – see Figure 14.

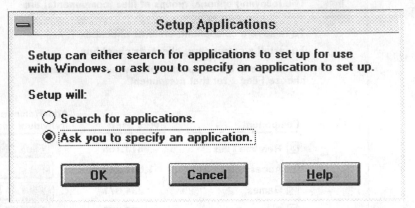

Figure 14

Choose the second option – 'Ask you to specify an application' and click OK.

3. The Setup Applications dialogue box appears – click the Browse button.

A list of Windows application programs appears – see Figure 15.

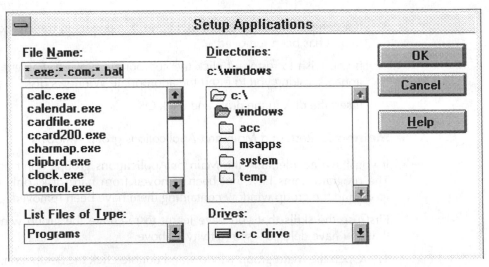

Figure 15

You will be able to recognise the names of the applications that you have removed. Click the program name then OK, eg CLOCK.EXE.

4. A further Setup Applications dialogue box appears.

   Click the down arrow button on the Add to Program Group box – a list of group windows appears – see Figure 16.

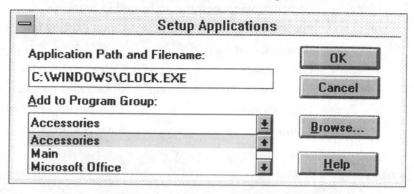

Figure 16

5. Click the appropriate group name than OK – the icon is restored to the appropriate group.

6. You will be returned to the Windows Setup dialogue box – stage 2 above.

   You will need to repeat the above operations for every application that you want to restore.

7. Finally exit Windows Setup.

Activity 7 Independent activity

Using the skills that you have gained in this unit carry out the following tasks:

1. Open the **Startup** group window and delete the two applications that you have added, Clock and Calendar.

   Do **not** remove any other applications from the Startup window unless you are authorised to do so.

2. Create a new Group Window entitled Desktop Accessories containing copies of the Calculator and Cardfile.

   It should resemble Appendix 1.

3. Finally delete the Desktop Accessories window.

Summary of menu commands

Notes

Menu commands show the menu name first, followed by the command to choose from the menu, e.g. Edit-Clear means open the Edit menu and select the Clear command. Where a command is available from a particular window this is indicated in brackets.

File – Open	Open existing file
(Program Manager)	
File – Delete	Delete group item
File – New – Program Group	Create new program group
File – Properties	Change properties of group item
Options – Save Settings on Exit	Save Windows settings formation Only)

unit 5
File Manager – organising your files

Introduction

You have already had a brief tour of File Manager in Unit 3.

This unit recaps on this and covers more advanced features.

What does File Manager do?

File Manager performs the basic 'housekeeping' tasks associated with organising and maintaining your files, you can :

Change from one disk drive to another

Change from one directory to another

Create a structure of directories

View the files that you have in a variety of ways – by size, date, type etc

Copy, rename, move and delete files

Format and copy whole disks.

You'll need to perform all these tasks sooner or later.

Do I need File Manager to perform these tasks?

It is possible to carry out at least some of the above tasks while you are using an application, or to use the MS-DOS file management features. However there will be situations when you are in Windows and want to review and tidy up your files – located perhaps in several directories or diskettes. In this situation File Manager is the quickest and easiest option to use. File Manager can also be used to print and to start up applications.

Skills covered	Activity
Directory – changing	1.8, 6
Directory levels – displaying	1.9
Drives – changing	1.6
Drive Windows – displaying	1.7
File Manager – starting	1.2
Files – sorting and viewing	2

Previous skills required	Covered in unit
Using the standard Windows components	1

Resources required

Practice files created in Unit 2

Activity 1 Fundamental ideas – files, directories and drives

This Activity introduces you to the the various parts of the File Manager window. Along the way it explains the key concepts of file, directory and drive.

1. Insert the diskette containing the practice files that you created in Unit 2 into the diskette drive. We will be using them in the activities that follow.

2. **Starting up File Manager.** Open the **Main** group window and then open **File Manager** – double click the File Manager icon.

   The window shown in Figure 1 appears.
   It contains the now familiar Windows features – title, menu and scroll bars, plus Maximise and Minimise buttons.

   On the desk top are icons representing files, directories and disk drives.
   Don't worry if yours differ from mine, we'll be working on ones that are common to all Windows systems.

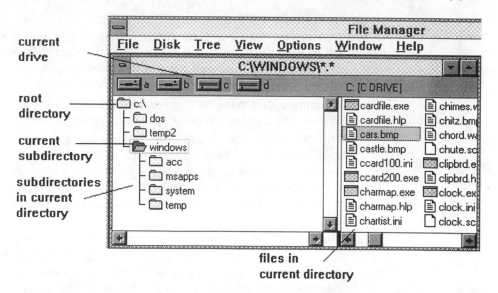

current drive
root directory
current subdirectory
subdirectories in current directory
files in current directory

Figure 1

3. **Troubleshooting.** If your display does not conform to this overall layout check that the following menu options are selected on the File Manager menu:

Tree   – Expand One Level

View   – Tree and Directory

        – Name

        – Sort by Name

These are the standard default settings for File Manager

4. **The Directory window.** When you open File Manager it is overlaid by the Directory window.

Along the top of the Directory window are various information items:

a.   the various drive icons – a, b, c etc

b.   to the right of these is the volume label – the name of the disk or network drive currently being read. If you look at Figure 1 above you will see that the drive currently selected is C. I have labelled it (C DRIVE). Yours may have no label, in which case only the drive letter C: will be shown.

c.   In the title bar of the Directory Window is the directory path – this shows the current directory, at present C:\WINDOWS*.* – this is discussed more fully in section 5d.

The main part of the window is split into two halves, the left side, showing your directories for the current drive, the right side showing the files in the current directory.

Drives, directories and files are your three basic units of organisation and we are going to take some time to explore them.

5. **Concepts and terminology**

   a. **Disk drives.** Your computer probably has at least two drives, the diskette drive, known as A drive, and the hard disk, known as C drive. You may well have other drives, e.g. you may be connected to a network or have a CD-ROM drive.

   Whenever you refer to a drive you do so using the letter followed by a colon symbol, e.g. a: or c: (upper or lower case)

   The diskette drive is used to store data in a portable form (ie on diskettes or floppy disks which can be removed) The hard disk and its drive unit are permanently fixed in the machine and holds MS-DOS, Windows and other applications, eg spreadsheet, word processor or database. It can also be used to store data.

   b. **Files.** Whatever you create on a computer has to be saved as a file. When you save a file you are copying information from the computer's main memory (RAM), which is temporary, to a permanent site on disk. If you did not save your work in this way it would be lost when the computer was turned off. A file on a computer is similar to a paper file in a filing cabinet. Both need a file name in order to file them away and retrieve them.

   c. **Rules for file names.** A file name can consist of up to 8 characters, these can be the letters A to Z (upper or lower case) or numbers 0 to 9.

   Certain other keyboard characters can be used, including the dash (-), and the underscore character. (_)

   The following *cannot* be used : space, comma, full stop, slash, colon, semicolon, brackets, quotation marks and the equals sign.

   The file name is usually followed by an extension of up to three characters, separated from the file name by a full stop or 'dot'. The extension usually identifies the type of file, and is often automatically allocated by the program which creates it. The different types of file are dealt with more fully in Activity 2

   d. **Directories.** A diskette can store dozens of files, a hard disk can store hundreds. To make files easier to locate they are placed into separate groups or directories – like drawers in a filing cabinet. There is a root or main directory, which is usually divided into further subdirectories. A typical structure is shown in Figure 1 above.

   It illustrates the tree structure adopted by Windows (and MS-DOS) The root directory is divided into 3 further directories, called subdirectories – DOS, TEMP2 and WINDOWS, each of which in their turn can be divided into further subdirectories, like branches on a tree.

   So each directory holds a collection of files and/or further subdirectories.

56

Let's see how the files and directories are stored on your disks. (Remember that they will be different to the ones on my computer)

6. **Changing drives.** Look at the disk icons displayed underneath the title bar. Click on the icon for c drive – it is outlined indicating that it is now the 'active' drive . Whenever you change drive a new drive window is displayed, showing the files and directories for that window. Only one drive can be active at one time.

   Click the **A** drive icon. A is now the active drive and is outlined with a rectangle.

   Look at the title of the desktop, it shows the new directory path – **A:*.***

   A: tells you that the disk currently in use is A, the floppy or diskette drive, *.* means 'all files'; the asterisk or star symbol is a 'wild card symbol' it can stand for any combination of characters – more of this in Unit 6.

   The files that you previously created on diskette should be displayed on the right side of the window. If not check that you have inserted the correct disk.

7. **Displaying multiple drive windows.** At the moment only the Window for A, the diskette is displayed.

   You may wish to display the window for C disk as well.

   Simply double click on the the C drive icon – the window for C drive is displayed, overlaying the A drive icon.

   Note: If this doesn't work change back to A drive and try again.

   This can be useful in comparing files on different disks. The windows can be moved or re-sized in the usual way – see Unit 1.

   Now double click on the C drive icon again; a duplicate (and unwanted) copy of the C drive window is made – see Figure 2

   Sometimes this may happen accidentally, usually because you have double clicked, rather than single clicked an icon. In this case simply close one of the copies of the C drive window in the usual way – double click the Control-menu box at the top left hand corner of the window – do this now.

   Now there are only two drive windows open, one for A and one for C.
   Close the Control-menu box to close the A drive window.
   Only the C drive window is open now.

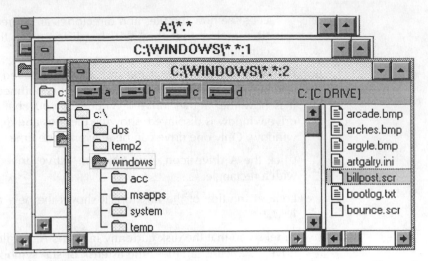

Figure 2

8. **Changing directories** Look at the directories on the left hand side of the window.

   First click on the directory labelled 'dos'. The files contained in the dos directory are displayed. Dos is selected as the 'current' directory, and the icon changes to show the directory as open.
   The title bar changes to show the new directory path **C:\DOS*.***

   Now click the Windows directory icon. The icon is highlighted and the files listed on the right of the window change. Each directory contains a different set of files.
   Some of the files necessary to run Windows are displayed – see Figure 3.

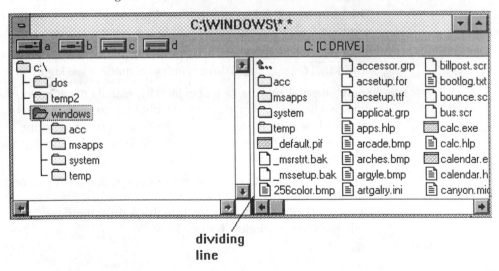

dividing
line

Figure 3

Scroll through the list. Some of them you will recognise, eg calendar.exe, clock.exe, notepad.exe.

58

Now double click on the Windows icon; you will find that the two windows subdirectories – System and Temp are displayed.

You will find that you can display more files at a time if you drag the dividing line between the two halves of the directory screen to the left (marked on figure 3) – don't overdo this

Now double click on the Dos directory icon – it contains files but no further subdirectories.

9. **Displaying subdirectories – the Tree menu.** The Tree menu at the top of the File Manager screen offers various ways of viewing the directory tree for your disk.

    Let's try each of these out in turn.

    Click once on the c:\ (root) directory icon – it is highlighted.

    Now open the **Tree** menu and select these options in turn:

    Collapse Branch – Shows the root directory, but no branches or subdirectories are shown. (this can also be done by double clicking a directory)

    Indicate Expandable Branches – The Windows directory, and any other directories with branches (i.e. subdirectories) are marked with a plus sign.
    The root directory c:\ is marked with a – sign to indicate that it contains subdirectories, but is currently open. This option is useful for finding out which directories have subdirectories. *This option can be de-selected later if you wish, but leave it selected for now.*

    Now select the Windows directory by clicking it once then select –

    Expand one level – The first layer of subdirectories in the Windows directory is displayed. (this is the equivalent of double clicking the directory icon)
    The Windows directory icon is now marked with a – sign, indicating that it has been expanded.

    Now double click on the C:\ root directory icon to collapse the directory tree.

    Expand all – All the branches/subdirectories in the root directory are shown; if there are many subdirectories on your hard disk then this display may be too crowded.

    Now select the Windows directory, then select,

    Expand branch – The subdirectory levels of a particular directory or subdirectory are displayed – in this case the Windows subdirectories System and Temp. If you look at the list of files on the right of the screen these two Windows subdirectories are listed, plus the files in the Windows directory.

    Now select **Collapse Branch** again to return you to the previous display, with no Windows subdirectories displayed.

59

Try double clicking on the Windows subdirectory a few times. The directory is either expanded or collapsed.

Activity 2   Viewing and sorting files – the View menu

In the previous activity we explored the three key file management ideas of,

Drive – your drive is used to either read information from or write information to your disk. Normally the drive is set to either your diskette in A drive or your internal hard disk – C drive.

Directory – every disk has a main or root directory; the root may divided into further subdirectories. This structure is called the directory tree.

File – Everything stored on disk is saved using a file name. Groups of related files are stored in directories.

In this activity we'll be finding out more about the different type of files. You'll also find out how to view them and sort them in different ways – by type, date, size etc.

1.   Make sure that the **File Manager** window is open.

If necessary enlarge both the File Manager window and the directory window so that a reasonable number of files can be viewed.

Select **C** drive and make sure that Windows is the current directory. The directory window should now be entitled 'C:\WINDOWS*.* This is the directory path and confirms that C is the current drive, Windows the current directory. The *.* symbol (called 'star dot star') indicates all files are being viewed.
The * is a ' wild card ' symbol, the first * means any characters may occur in the file name, the second * that any characters may occur in the file extension.
The \ or backslash symbol represents levels of directory and subdirectory; as indicated in Figure 4 there are 2 backslashes to show the root directory containing the Windows subdirectory.

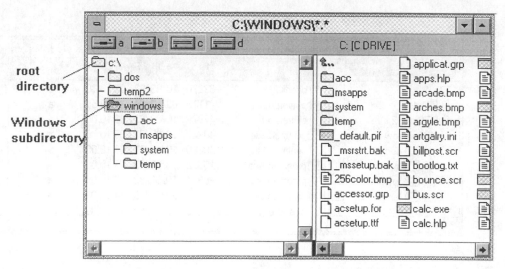

root directory

Windows subdirectory

Figure 4

2. **The View menu**

   Using the View menu at the top of the screen, we can view the files in a variety of ways.

   First try out the first four options on the View menu in turn:

   Tree and directory is the default setting for the directory window, it should already be selected (ticked); on the left side is the directory tree, and on the right side any files and subdirectories in the current directory. This is normally the most useful display.

   Tree Only shows the directory tree only without the files it contains.

   Directory Only shows the files in the current directory, but not the directory tree.

   Re-select the first option – Tree and directory

   Split allows you to shift the dividing line between the two halves of the window. Select this option and a thick line appears; use the screen pointer to move it to a new location then click to place it there.

3. **File details**

   Open the **View** menu again. The next section of the menu shows three options – Name, All File Details and Partial Details.
   These options controls the amount of detail displayed on each file;

   Name – at the moment the default option Name is selected (ticked) and only the file names are shown. This permits the maximum number of files to be viewed in the window.

   All file details – select this option and a display resembling Figure 5 appears

61

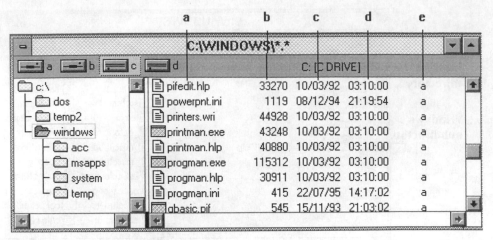

Figure 5

They have been labelled a – e for reference

a. The file icon and name. Notice that the icon design and the extension both help to indicate the type of file, eg:

.wri – a Windows Write file

.exe – a program file

b. The file size in bytes. One byte holds the equivalent of a character, eg a keyboard character such as), 0 or c, as well as special characters normally invisible to the user. In an executable program file a byte holds one machine instruction. A kilobyte or 1K is roughly 1,000 bytes (actually 1024 bytes), a megabyte or Mb equals a million bytes.

Also note that along the bottom of the window is shown the size of the file currently selected, (if any) the total size of the current disk, plus the total number of files in the current directory.

c. and d. The date and time that the file was created or last modified. Many files will share the same date and time – when they were first installed on disk.

e. The file attributes. These control the kind of operations you can carry out on a file. The a means that the file has an archive attribute. We will look at attributes in more detail in Unit 7.

4. Sorting files

The next section of the View menu offers a number of sort options. Sort by Name is the default option – the files on disk are in alphabetic order of file name.

Now try these Sort by options on the View menu

Sort by type – the files are sorted into order of their extension, eg all .HLP (help) files are grouped together – see Figure 6.

62

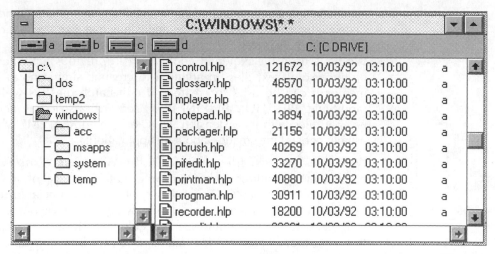

Figure 6

Directories are always listed first in alphabetical order, then a number of different file types are listed – this may be a good time to review them. Scroll through the list of files and identify files ending in the following extensions:

.COM is a short program or command file.

.EXE files are also program files – double clicking them EXEcutes or runs them. Normally it is easier to run them from their group window such as the Accessories or Main group windows, but using File Manager is useful if you cannot locate the program.

.GRP files represent the various group windows; e.g. startup.grp represents the startup group window.

.HLP files contain the help text for various applications, e.g. calendar.hlp contains the help text for the calendar applications. Normally these files are called by taking the Help option from the particular application.

.INI files are initialisation files They contain text that holds the information to set up Windows to run in a particular way; we have already looked at the progman.ini file that controls the Program Manager window in Unit 4.

.PIF files are Program Identification Files; they contain the text instructions for Windows to run a non-Windows application such as MS-DOS.

.SCR files contain screen savers; these are moving patterns that overlay the normal screen display if the PC has not been used for some preset time. Pressing any key will return you to the normal display. This may already have been installed on your computer.

.TXT files are text files. They contain only the basic keyboard characters a to z and 0 to 9, plus puctuation marks and other typable keyboard chatracters.

63

Notepad files are also referred to as ASCII files (American Standard Code for Information Interchange), indicating that they contain only the standard characters.

We have used the Notepad application in previous activities to produce some text files. In addition to creating simple notes and memos it can be used to create and edit batch files, as well as modifying .PIF, .HLP, and .INI files. You will also come across notepad files with the extension .DOC or named READ.ME which usually contain information about an application.

.WRI files are text files created in the Windows Write word processor. You will remember that we used this application in Unit 2. Unlike the Notepad .TXT files they contain many special (usually invisible) characters that control the appearance and layout of the text, e.g. bold, font size, line spacing, columns. These are essential to create more complex documents, but vary between different word processors.

Sort by size. The files are displayed in descending order of size.

The 'All File Details' option should still be selected.

Sort by Date. The files are displayed in their order of creation.

5. **Viewing different types of files**

    Take the final option on the View menu – **by File type.**

    A dialogue box appears – see Figure 7.

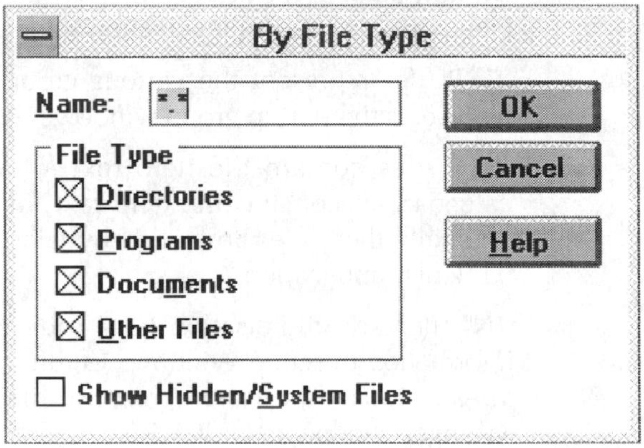

Figure 7

This option allows you to select which type of file – Directories, Programs, Documents or Other files – you want to display. At the moment all files are selected by default, ie the boxes are marked with a cross

Experiment with deselecting some of these options.

First deselect the **Documents** option and the **Other Files** option, then click **OK.**

Now open the **View** menu again and select **Sort by Type.**

64

Scroll through the list of files.

First subdirectories are displayed, then three groups of program files are displayed- files ending in the extension COM, EXE and PIF.

6. Now open the **View** menu and select the **by File Type** option again.

   This time re-select the **Documents** and **Other Files** options and deselect the first two options – Directories and Programs. Click **OK.**

   A different set of files is displayed.

   Select the **by File Type** option again and re-select all four options. Leave the dialogue box open

7. **Searching by extension**

   If you wish to view one particular kind of file then it is possible to type its extension in the Name box.

   At the moment the Name box displays the *.* ('star dot star') meaning all file names and all extensions are selected. Amend it to *.TXT – meaning any file with the .TXT extension – and click OK. All text files in the Windows directory are listed.

   Now select some another directory, eg DOS, and any text files that they contain will be listed – try this.

   Finally re-select the Windows directory and carry on with the next activity.

8. **Independent activity**

   Make sure that the Windows directory is the current directory. Open the **View** menu and make sure that the **Sort by Type** option is selected.

   Find a couple of examples of each of the following type of file, and call them up by double-clicking the icon:

   a. .EXE files – the application will run

   b. .HLP file – the help text is displayed

   c. .TXT file – a notepad document is displayed

   d. .WRI file – a Write document is displayed

   As you have seen, File Manager provides a quick and easy way of finding files on disk; once you have located a file you can open it directly from File Manager.

Summary of menu commands

Notes

Menu commands show the menu name first, followed by the command to choose from the menu, e.g. Edit-Clear means open the Edit menu and select the Clear command. Where a command is available from a particular window this is indicated in brackets.

(File Manager)

Tree – Collapse Branch	Show root directory only
Tree – Indicate Expandable Branches	Show directories containing other directories
Tree – Expand All	Show all subdirectories
Tree – Expand Branch	Show subdirectories of selected directory
Tree – Expand One Level	Show first layer of subdirectories
View – All File Details	View all details of files displayed
View – Directory Only	Show only files in current directory
View – Name	Only names of files shown
View – Sort by...	Display files in different orders
View – Tree	Show only directory tree
View – Tree and Directory	Show both files and subdirectories
Window – New Window	Display a new window

unit 6
Moving and copying files

Introduction

In this unit we will be reorganising the practice files that we created in Unit 2. We will move or copy them into two directories called SALES and ACCOUNTS.

Skills covered	Activity
Directory – deleting	1.5,
Directory – making and renaming	1
Files – copying and moving	2, 3, 5

Previous skills required	Covered in unit
Using the standard Windows components	1

Resources required

Practice files created in Unit 2

Activity 1   Making and renaming directories

In unit 2 we created 16 dummy files, eight using the Notepad text editor application (extension .TXT), and eight using the Write word processor application (extension .WRI). These are:

MEMSAL1.TXT

MEMSAL2.TXT

MEMSAL3.TXT

MEMSAL4.TXT

MEMACC1.TXT

MEMACC2.TXT

MEMACC3.TXT

67

MEMACC4.TXT

LETSAL1.JM

LETSAL2.WRI

LETSAL3.WRI

LETSAL4.WRI

LETACC1.WRI

LETACC2.WRI

LETACC3.WRI

LETACC4.WRI

The file names contain 4 elements :

The first three letters indicate the type of document, MEM = memo, LET = letter.

letters 4 – 6 indicate the department, ACC = Accounts and SAL = Sales.

The final digit, 1,2,3 etc. on the file name indicates the order of creation and ensures that each file name is unique.

The file name is separated by a full stop from an optional 3 letter extension.

We are going to organise these files into directories and subdirectories; all the files concerned with Sales Department will be placed in a directory SALES and those concerned with the Accounts Department in a directory ACCOUNTS. The directory tree will look like Figure 1:

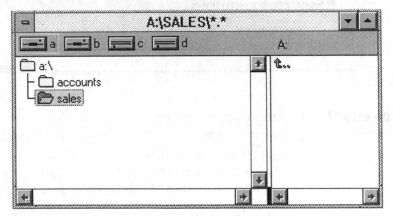

Figure 1

Notes on directory names

Directory names follow the same conventions as file names, except that directories cannot have an extension, ie:

A directory name can consist of up to 8 characters, these can be the letters A to Z (upper or lower case) or numbers 0 to 9.

Certain other keyboard characters can be used, including the dash (-), and the underscore character (_).

The following *cannot* be used : space, comma, full stop, slash, colon, semicolon, brackets, quotation marks and the equals sign.

You may succeed in creating directories with these invalid characters, but you are liable to lose some of the characters from the name and unpredictable results may occur when you use them.

1. Make sure that the diskette containing the above files is inserted in A drive.

   Open **File Manager** and ensure that A is the active drive (click once on the icon for a: drive, top left of the window). The Directory window should resemble Figure 2.

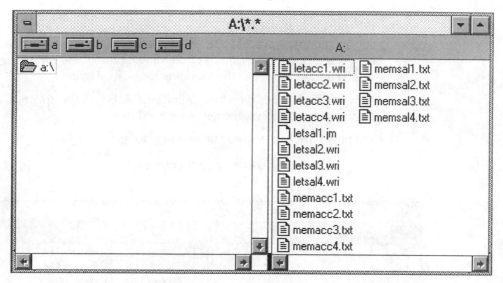

Figure 2

If the files are not displayed, check that the correct diskette is in a drive; if no files at all are displayed open the **View** menu and make sure that the **Tree and Directory** option is selected.

2. **Creating a directory**

   Open the **File** menu and select the **Create Directory** option.

   A dialogue box appears – see Figure 3.

   Check that the current directory is A:\ The drive is A, the colon (:) symbol always follows the drive letter, the backslash (\) symbol represents the root directory – the main directory on a disk that contains all the files and other directories. If the path is incorrect then click the Cancel button and make drive A the active drive – see section 1.

69

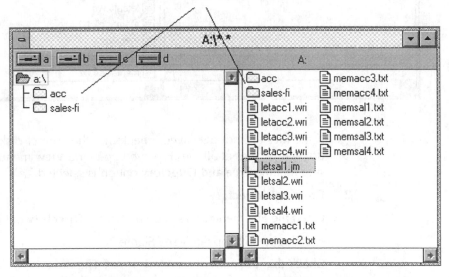

Figure 3

3. To test the rules for directory names (see above) let's try typing invalid names. Enter the directory name SALES-FILES in the **Name** box and click **OK**.

A new directory called SALES-FI is created in the root directory. Windows has given the directory the first 8 characters of the name and ignored the rest. SALES-FI is displayed both on the left side of the Directory window as part of the directory tree and on the right side as a subdirectory in the root directory – see Figure 4.

Now create another directory called ACC DIR. As the space is an invalid character the name gets shortened to ACC

We now have two wrongly named directories!

newly created subdirectories

Figure 4

4. **Renaming directories**

We can now either rename a directory or remove it and re-create it. Let's rename one first.

Click the SALES-FI directory once to select it.

70

Open the **File** menu and select **Rename.** A dialogue box appears – see Figure 5.

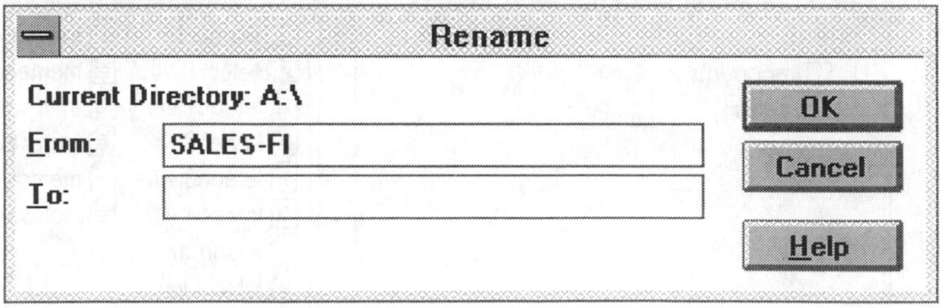

Rename

Current Directory: A:\

From: SALES-FI

To:

OK

Cancel

Help

Figure 5

Enter the new name SALES in the To: box and click **OK.** The directory is renamed.

All directories can be renamed in this way, except for the root directory.

5. **Removing directories**

Click the ACC directory once to select it.

Open the **File** menu and select **Delete.** A dialogue box appears – see Figure 6.

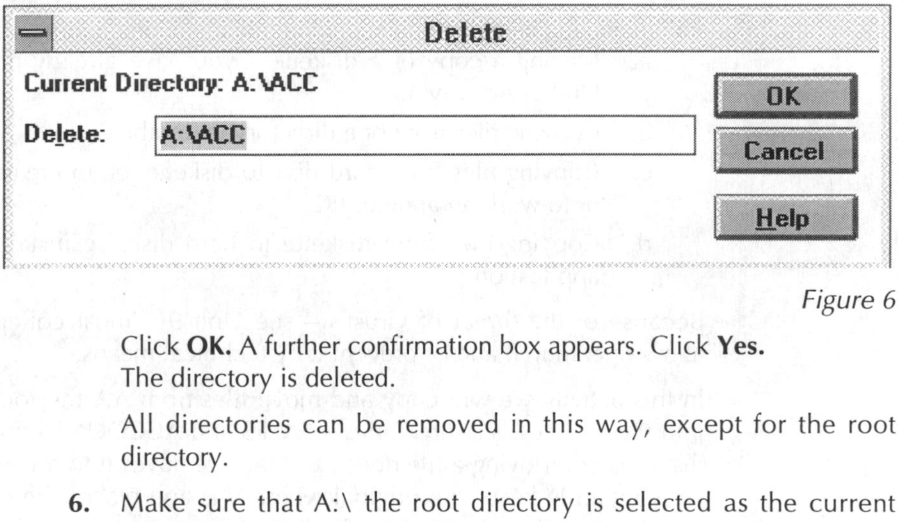

Delete

Current Directory: A:\ACC

Delete: A:\ACC

OK

Cancel

Help

Figure 6

Click **OK.** A further confirmation box appears. Click **Yes.** The directory is deleted.

All directories can be removed in this way, except for the root directory.

6. Make sure that A:\ the root directory is selected as the current directory and create a second directory ACCOUNTS (see section 2 above if necessary). The Directory window should now resemble Figure 7.

7. Select each new subdirectory (SALES and ACCOUNTS) in turn – no files or directories are displayed on the right hand side of the screen – as yet there are no files in these subdirectories.

Select the root directory a:\ again

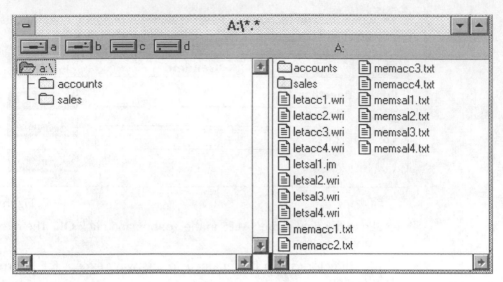

Figure7

Activity 2   Moving and copying individual files

Copying and moving files are essential procedures, typical situations are:

a.   Making a copy of a diskette – you have already done this in Unit 3, Activity 4.

b.   Copying files from one directory to another.

c.   Copying files from hard disk to diskette, eg to create backups, or to work on another PC.

d.   Copying files from diskette to hard disk, eg installing a new application.

Because of the threat of viruses – see Unit 9 – most colleges do not allow operation d and/or prevent it by technical means.

In this activity we will copy and move files from A:\ the root directory into the two new subdirectories – SALES and ACCOUNTS that we have just created. Moving a file does just that – removes it to a new location, copying a file keeps the original where it is and places the copy in the new location. We will practice both operations.

You can either use the mouse to 'drag and drop' the file in its new location or use the Copy and Move commands.

1.   Copying files

Make sure that the diskette containing the above files is inserted in A drive.

72

Open File Manager and ensure that A is the active drive (click once on the icon for a: drive, top left of the window). The Directory window should resemble Figure 8.

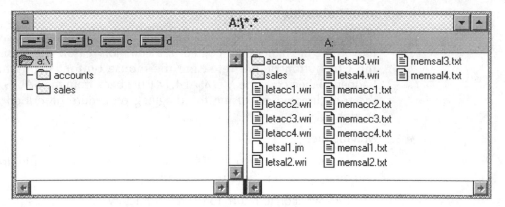

Figure 8

2. Hold down the **Ctrl** key and move the cursor onto the file MEMSAL4.TXT

   Hold down the mouse button and drag the file on top of the icon for the SALES directory. – see Figure 9.

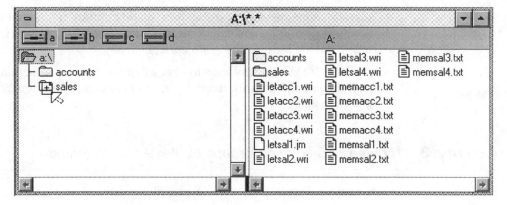

Figure 9

The cursor changes to a file icon with a plus sign – this indicates that the file is being copied rather than moved.

Now keep the Ctrl key pressed down and release the mouse button. The file drops into the SALES directory.
A confirmation message appears; this should confirm the file name, the copying operation, and the destination – the SALES directory. Check all these before you click the Yes button. (nb if you released the Ctrl key too soon then the file will be moved rather than copied. In this case click the No button to cancel the operation and try again)

3. Click the icon for the SALES directory to check that the the file has actually been copied and the root directory to check that the original is still there.

4. **Troubleshooting**

   If the original is missing from the root directory then you have moved the file rather than copied it; a common reason is releasing the Ctrl button *before* releasing the mouse button. If this has happened then copy the MEMSAL4.TXT file back from the SALES to the root directory a:\ using the dragging procedure described in section 2.

5. **Moving files**

   Now try *moving* a file to the SALES subdirectory. It is a simple drag and drop operation; the Ctrl key is not used.

   Click the a:\ icon to return to the root directory

   Now move the screen pointer onto the file MEMSAL3.TXT.

   Hold down the mouse button and drag the file on top of the icon for the SALES directory.

   Release the mouse button and the file drops into the SALES directory.

   A confirmation message appears; this should confirm the file name, the move operation, and the destination directory SALES. Click OK only if you are satisfied these are correct.

   Click the SALES directory icon to check that the the file has actually been moved and the root directory a:\ to check that the original is no longer there.

Activity 3   Moving and copying groups of files – mouse method

1. Now we will copy and move several files at once.

   If necessary make sure that the diskette containing the practice files is still inserted in A drive, open File Manager and check that the root directory a:\ is selected.

2. **Copying groups of files**

   First we will copy some of the file names starting with the characters LETSAL from the root directory to the SALES subdirectory.

   Hold down the Ctrl key and click the following three file names: LETSAL1.JM, LETSAL2.WRI and LETSAL3.WRI.
   All three file names should now be highlighted. If you select the wrong file name simply click it to de-select it.

   Next, *keeping the Ctrl key pressed down,* keep the pointer on the block of files that you have selected and drag these files onto the

SALES directory icon and release the mouse button then the Ctrl key.

A confirmation message appears; this should confirm the copying operation and the destination – the SALES directory. Check these before you click the Yes button. (nb if you released the Ctrl key too soon then the files will be moved rather than copied. In this case click the No button to cancel the operation and try again.)

3. Click the SALES directory icon to check that the the three files have actually been copied and the root directory to check that the originals are still there.

    If the originals are missing from the root directory then you have moved the files rather than copied them; a common reason is releasing the Ctrl button *before* releasing the mouse button. If this has happened then copy the files back from the SALES to the root directory a:\ using the dragging procedure described in section 2.

4. **Moving groups of files**

    We will move some more files starting with the characters LETSAL from the root directory to the SALES subdirectory.

    Hold down the Ctrl key and click the following three file names: MEMSAL1, MEMSAL2.TXT and LETSAL4.WRI.

    All three file names should be highlighted now. If you select the wrong file name simply click it to de-select it.

    Now *release* the Ctrl key – if you omit this step the files will be copied rather than moved.

    Keep the pointer on one of the files in the block of files that you have selected and drag these files onto the SALES icon.

    Release the mouse button.

    A confirmation message appears; this should confirm the move operation and the destination – the SALES directory. Check these before you click the Yes button.

5. Click the SALES directory icon to check that the the three files are now in this directory and the root directory to check that they have been moved.
    All 8 files with SAL in their file names should now be in the SALES subdirectory – see Figure 10; they have been moved or copied there from the root directory. Check this and move or copy them if they are not there.

    Troubleshooting. Look in the ACCOUNTS subdirectory as well as the root directory; the ACCOUNTS should be empty; if they contain files with SAL in their file names then copy them into the SALES subdirectory.

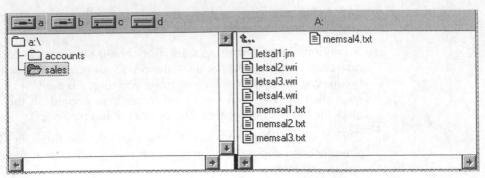

Figure 10

Activity 4   Displaying two directories

In this activity you will learn how to open more than one directory window at the same time using the New Window command. This is useful if you want to check and compare the contents of two directories before moving or copying.

If necessary make sure that the diskette containing the practice files is inserted in A drive, open File Manager and check that the root directory a:\ is selected.

1. Click the icon for the SALES subdirectory – it opens displaying the files.

    Now click the icon for the ACCOUNTS subdirectory; the SALES subdirectory is closed and ACCOUNTS opened.

    Try this a few times – only one directory can be open at once.

2. Now open the ACCOUNTS subdirectory.

    Open the **Window** menu and select the option **New Window.**

    A second copy of the ACCOUNTS subdirectory, entitled A:\ACCOUNTS*.*2 is opened – see Figure 11.

    It overlays the original window.

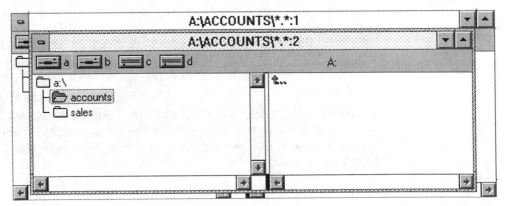

Figure 11

76

3. Move the pointer onto the icon for the SALES subdirectory and click. The duplicate ACCOUNTS window is changed to a window for the SALES subdirectory – see Figure 12.

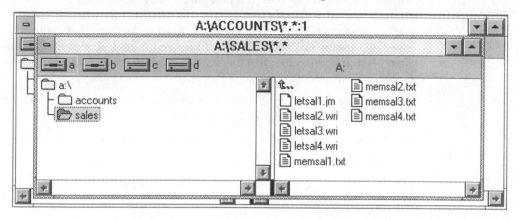

Figure 12

4. Open the **Window** menu, two windows are listed, one for SALES and one for ACCOUNTS – check this.

   Select **Tile** from the Window menu and both windows are visible.

   The two windows can be made smaller if necessary so that all files are visible – see Figure 13.

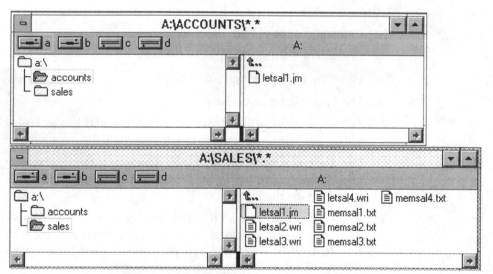

Figure 13

The tiled display allows you compare their contents and to copy or move files in the usual way.

5. Copy the file LETSAL1.JM from the SALES to the ACCOUNTS subdirectory using the Ctrl key and 'dragging'.

77

Activity 5 Copying and moving groups of files – menu method

If there is a long list of files in a directory it may be difficult to locate the all the files that you want to copy. In this case you may find it easier to use the Move or Copy commands on the File menu. This method is especially useful in copying files with related names. The only complication is that you need to use the 'wild card' characters * and ? to represent files with similar names.

To learn more about wild cards consult unit 11. For the moment the following rules and examples will be enough:

The * or 'star' can stand for any number of characters; eg:

*.WRI means any file name ending in the extension .WRI

LET*.* means a file name starting with the the three characters LET and ending in anything.

. signifies all files (any name, any extension)

The ? symbol substitutes for individual characters; suppose that I want to find all file names containing the three characters ACC in positions 4 to 6 of the file name, e.g. MEMACC1.TXT or LETACC2.WRI. I need to locate the wild card symbols at character positions 4 to 6. So the file name ???ACC?.* means 'starting with any three characters, then the characters ACC, any other character at the end, and followed by any extension (*)'

1. **Copying groups of files**

   Check that the root directory A:\ is selected.

   Open the **File** menu and select **Copy.**

   The Copy Dialogue box appears.

2. The name of the current directory, A:\ is listed in the **From:** box. This is our *source* directory – the directory we are copying from.

   The **To:** box is for the *destination* directory – the directory we are copying to. If you want to read more on these then click the Help button on the dialogue box.

3. We are going to copy all the files concerned with accounts into the ACCOUNTS subdirectory; as previously mentioned (see introduction to Unit 6, Activity 3) all accounts-related files contain the letters ACC at positions 4-6 of the file name.

4. Position the screen pointer after the A: in the From: box and click.

   Type the file name **???ACC?.*** – see Figure 14.

   Take care to get each character exactly as shown!

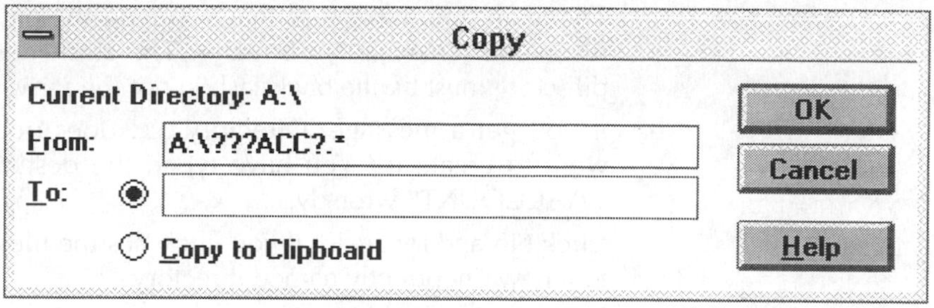

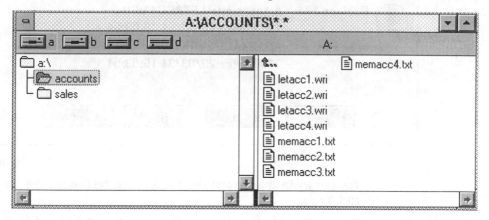

Figure 14

5. We are copying all these files to the ACCOUNTS subdirectory.

   Click the **To:** box and type the name of the destination directory **A:\ACCOUNTS** – see Figure 15.

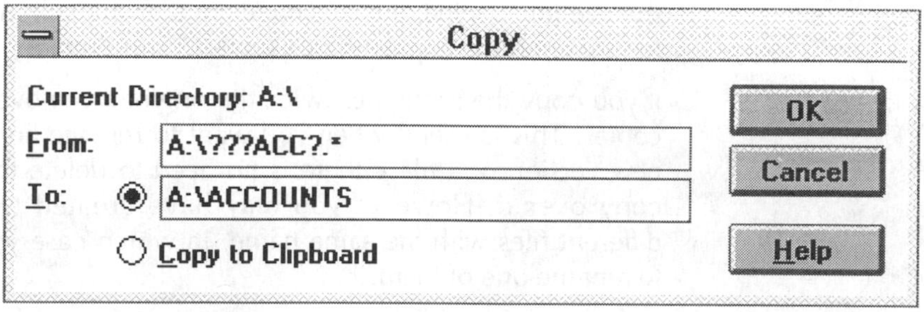

Figure 15

Now click **OK.** A dialogue box should confirm that copying is taking place.

If so open the ACCOUNTS subdirectory and check that the eight files have been copied – see Figure 16.

Figure 16

6. **Troubleshooting**

   a. If you get a message 'Cannot Copy ..... Cannot Find File....'then you have probably specified the source files incorrectly.

Try again and make sure that you type the path (A:\) and the file name (???ACC?.*) correctly. The slash denoting the root directory must be the backslash(\) not the forward slash (/).

b. If you get a message 'Directory ..... does not exist. Do you want to create it?' You have typed the destination directory A:\ACCOUNTS wrongly.

Click No and try again. If you click Yes the files will be copied to a new, incorrectly named directory.

7. **Copying the same file more than once**

You may wonder what would happen if we copied the same files again; would we create files with identical names in the same directory? The answer is no! Windows only permits identical file names in different directories. (we have this situation with the files that we just copied, the original eight files are still in the root directory A:\ and the copies in ACCOUNTS subdirectory)

If you copy the same files twice the originals are overwritten by the copies. This is useful when you want to replace an original with a new version of a file – there is no need to delete the original, just copy over it. However you may have created two completely different files with the same name, in which case you would need to rename one of them.

To make this point repeat the copy command above – see sections 4 and 5. This time you are warned that the original copies in the ACCOUNTS subdirectory will be overwritten – see Figure 17.

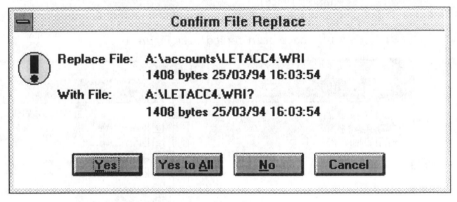

Figure 17

You can tell by the size and creation date that the two files are identical, click **Yes.**

The next file to be copied is confirmed; if you are satisfied click **Yes** again.

This process will continue until all the original copies are replaced.

Click **No** if for any reason you do not want the original overwritten.

Click **'Yes to All'** if you want all the originals overwritten without further confirmation messages.

8. **Moving files using the Move command**. We will not practise this command specifically as it is exactly the same principle as the Copy command that we have just carried out.

Summary of menu commands

Notes

Menu commands show the menu name first, followed by the command to choose from the menu, e.g. Edit-Clear means open the Edit menu and select the Clear command. Where a command is available from a particular window this is indicated in brackets.

(File Manager)

File – Copy	Copy file
File – Create Directory	Create a new directory
File – Delete	Delete a file or directory
File – Move	Move file
File – Rename	Rename file or directory
View – Tree and Directory	Show both files and subdirectories
Window – New Window	Display a new window

Other File Manager operations

Introduction

In this unit you will be learning how to rename and delete files and directories, how to display hidden files and how to create a system disk.

Skills covered	Activity
Directory – deleting	4
Files – associating with an application	2
Files – deleting	3
Files – renaming	1
Hidden Files – displaying	6
System Disk – creating	5

Previous skills required	Covered in unit
Using the standard Windows components	1

Resources required

Practice files created in Unit 2

Activity 1 Renaming files

Often we need to need to change the name of a file, perhaps because it is incorrect, or to distinguish it from an earlier or later version. We can either rename it or copy it under another name. We will try both of these.

1. **Renaming a file without copying.** If necessary make sure that the diskette containing the practice files is still inserted in A drive, open File Manager and check that the root directory a:\ is selected.

   Open the SALES subdirectory and select the file LETSAL1.JM (click it once)

We will give it the extension .WRI to identify it as a Windows Write file.

2. Open the **File** menu and select the **Rename** option – the Rename dialogue box appears – see Figure 1.

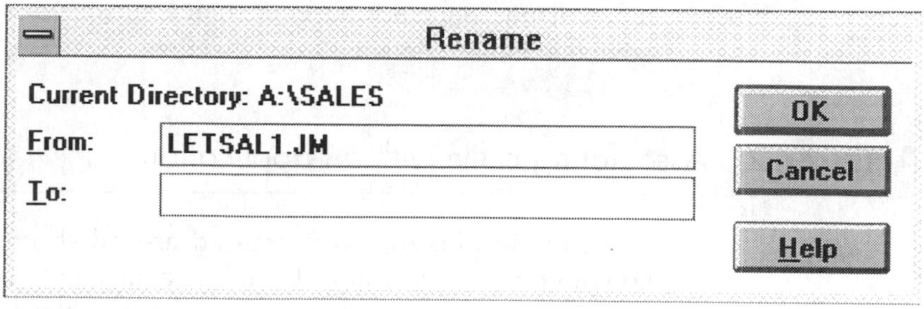

Figure 1

The directory path A:\SALES and the current file name LETSAL1.JM are already entered.

Click the **To:** box and enter the new name LETSAL1.WRI

Click the **OK** button and the file is renamed – check the directory listing to confirm this.

You will also notice that the icon for this file is now the same as the other files with the extension .WRI. Windows is now able to recognise the file as a Write file and associate it with the Windows Write application.

We will be looking in more detail at associating data files with applications in Activity 2.

3. **Copying and re-naming.**

Let's copy the file MEMACC4.TXT from the ACCOUNTS to the SALES subdirectory, re-naming it MEMSAL5.TXT.

Open the ACCOUNTS subdirectory and select the file MEMACC4.TXT.

Now open the **File** menu and select the **Copy** option. The Copy dialogue box appears – see Figure 2.

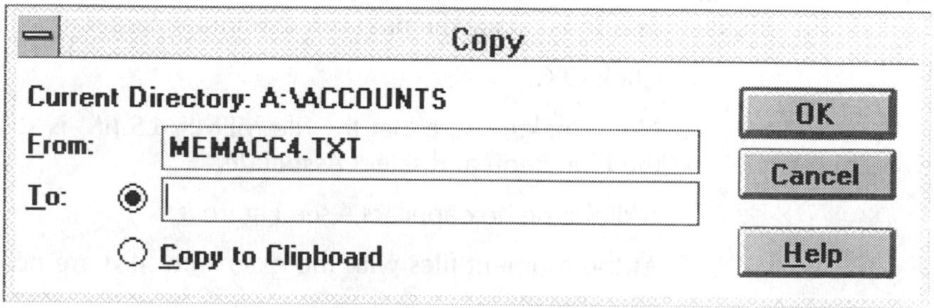

Figure 2

The directory path A:\ACCOUNTS and the source file name MEMACC4.TXT are already entered.

Click the **To:** box and enter the destination directory and new file name A:\SALES\MEMSAL5.JIM

Click **OK** and the file is copied and re-named.

Open the SALES subdirectory and check that the renamed file is there. If this does not happen then consult the trouble shooting advice in Unit 6, Activity 5.

Activity 2 Associating a file with an application

The sample files that you created are all short data files, they contain text – mainly alphabetic characters and numbers. The files with the extension .TXT were created in Notepad, the Windows text editor, files with the extension .WRI were created in Write, the Windows word processor. This saves time when you want to retrieve a file; you have no need to start the application and then open the file – opening the file automatically starts the associated application. If data files are not given the standard default extension then Windows cannot automatically associate them with the software package (i.e. the program) that created them. This means that when you try to open the file directly from File Manager you will get an error message. In this case you must tell Windows which program is associated with the data file.

We have one file without a standard extension, MEMSAL5.JIM However we can associate a data file with its application without needing to alter the extension to a standard one.

1. Open the SALES subdirectory and double click the file LETSAL2.WRI

    The Write application starts automatically. Windows can associate the file with the Windows Write application because of its .WRI extension.

    Exit from the document back to File Manager – the file and its associated program is closed.

2. Now double click the file MEMSAL5.JIM. An error message will inform you that the program cannot be run.

    Click **OK.**

    Now, making sure that the file MEMSAL5.JIM is still selected, open the **File** menu and select **Associate.**

    A dialogue box appears – see Figure 3.

    At the moment files with the extension .JIM are not associated with an application.

    Scroll down the list of files until you reach the bottom.

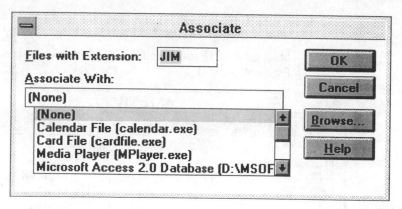

Figure 3

Select the option **Text File** and click **OK.**

The icon for MEMSAL5.JIM changes to a standard Notepad document; double click it and the the Notepad application starts automatically. Windows can now associate the file with the Notepad application.

Exit from the document back to File Manager – the file and its associated program is closed.

Activity 3 Deleting files

Files can be deleted using the Delete command on the File menu. The files can be identified either by,

a. first selecting them using the mouse then using the Delete option, or,

b. selecting the Delete option first then typing in the file or directory names.

Before a file is deleted you will be asked to confirm it, this is very important, in Windows 3.1 as files cannot be undeleted (although they can in MS-DOS and Windows 95)

1. If necessary make sure that the diskette containing the practice files is still inserted in A drive, open File Manager and check that the root directory a:\ is selected.

First let's create a directory with some files in it for us to practise deletion. It will be in the root directory and be named TEST.

First select A:\ the root directory.

Open the **File** menu and select **Create directory.**

Enter the name TEST in the dialogue box and click **OK.**

The new directory is listed in the directory tree.

85

2. Now, using the operations that you learnt in Unit 6, copy all the files from SALES to the TEST subdirectory.

3. Select the TEST subdirectory; check that you have the files listed in Figure 4.

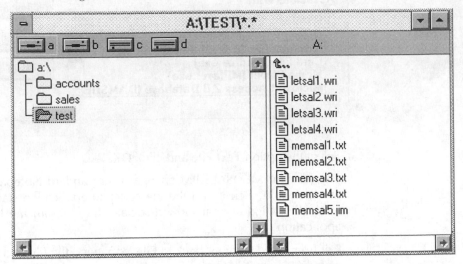

Figure 4

If not you will need to copy them over again.

4. **Deleting individual files.** Select the file LETSAL1.WRI

   Open the **File** menu and select **Delete.**

   The following dialogue box appears, confirming the file that you have specified for deletion.

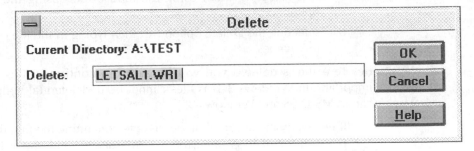

You are offered three options, OK, Cancel or Help.

Select the **OK** option and the Confirm File Delete dialogue box is displayed.

Click the **Yes** button and the file LETSAL1.WRI is deleted – check this in the directory listing.

5. **Deleting several files – Mouse method.** Hold down the **Ctrl** key and select files MEMSAL1.TXT and MEMSAL2.TXT.

   Open the **File** menu and select **Delete.**

The dialogue box appears, confirming the two files that you have specified for deletion.

Click **OK** and a further dialogue box appears asking you to confirm each file deletion – see Figure 5.

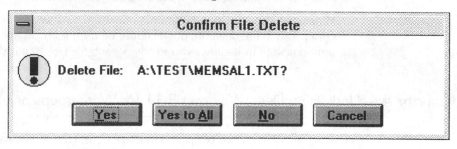

Figure 5

Select the **Yes** option and the first file is deleted, the dialogue box appears again, asking you to confirm the second deletion, Select the Yes option again.

The two files MEMSAL1.TXT and MEMSAL2.TXT have been deleted – check this in the directory listing.

6. **Deleting several files – menu method.** You learnt in Unit 6 that it is quicker to use wildcard operators * and ? to specify a list of files with similar names.

   We will delete the remaining files with the .TXT extension.

   Make sure that no files are currently selected.

   Open the **File** menu and select **Delete.**

   When the dialogue box appears only the directory name A:\TEST should be listed – see Figure 6.

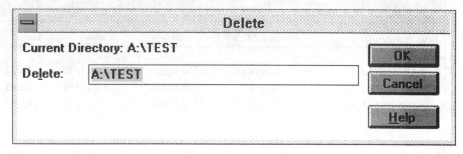

Figure 6

If a file name is selected then take the Cancel option, deselect the file (Ctrl key and click) and try again.

Now amend the entry in the Delete box to **A:\TEST*.TXT**

*.TXT means 'all file names ending in .TXT

TEST\ means 'in the TEST directory'

A:\ means 'in the root directory on A drive'

Click the **OK** button.

The second dialogue box appears, asking you to confirm each file deletion in turn. This time click the **Yes to All** button.

All the files will be deleted without further confirmation.

Warning. The Yes to All option saves time as there is no need to confirm each file deletion, but it should be used with caution. The Yes option is safer as it allows you to check each file before it is deleted.

Activity 4 Undeleting files. (Windows 3.11 for Workgroups only)

Windows for Workgroups offers an Undelete command in File Manager. It can be used to recover specific directories, files or a group of files. A file is deleted by deleting the first character of the file name so there is no directory reference to it in the File Allocation Table. Eventually the file is overwritten by new data – unless it is promptly recovered. This facility should not be used as a substitute for taking regular backups! UNDELETE cannot for example restore a deleted file if it was in a deleted subdirectory.

1. Make sure that the diskette containing the practice files is still inserted in A drive, that File Manager is open and check that the TEST directory on a: drive is selected.

2. Open the **File** menu and select **Undelete.** A dialogue box appears listing the files deleted in the previous activity – see Figure 7.

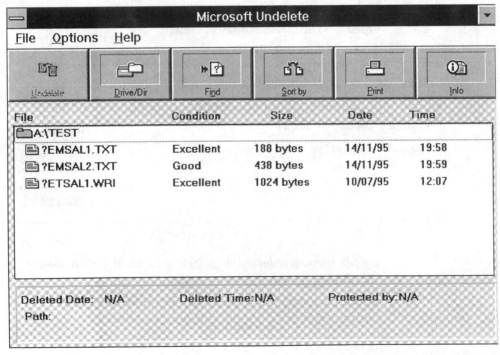

Figure 7

Notice that the first character of the filename is replaced by a ? If you have previously used the disk for other activities then you may well see other deleted files listed.

Various buttons appear along the top of the dialogue box:

Drive/Dir Search for deleted files on other drives or directories

Find Seach for deleted files by name/wild card search

Sort by Sort list of deleted files (good for long lists)

Print Print list of deleted files (good for long lists)

Info Get more information on a deleted file (try this)

3. **File condition**

    You will see that each file is listed as good, perfect, etc.

    Press the F1 key to find out more about this. You will learn that only files protected by the MS-DOS Delete Sentry utility can be perfect – see MS-DOS units on UNDELETE and DEFRAG commands.

    'Excellent' condition files have all their sections or clusters complete and unfragmented, ie all stored in one disk location rather than scattered over the disk. 'Good' files are complete but fragmented etc.

4. Select the first deleted file in the list, eg ?EMSAL1.TXT, and click the **Undelete** button.You are prompted to provide the first character of the file name.

    Type, eg, M and click **OK**.

    If you are successful the file is marked 'Recovered'. Sometimes a file cannot be undeleted because another file has overwritten part of the deleted file. If so it will be marked 'Destroyed' , You could try to recover it using the MS-DOS undelete command – read section 6 below.

5. Now use the mouse and the **Ctrl** key to select the remaining deleted files and then attempt to undelete them.

6. **Note – higher levels of file recovery.**

    The UNDELETE command in MS-DOS 5 also offers Tracker, a deletion-tracking file, this file note the names of up to 200 deleted files, saving you the effort of remembering the first character of the filename. The MIRROR command is used to load Tracker. Tracker cannot recover files where the space occupied by the deleted files has already been re-used.

    MS-DOS 6 offers Sentry which keeps deleted files in a special hidden subdirectory, SENTRY, which is virtually impossible to delete.

    These two higher levels are especially appropriate to a hard disk if accidental deletion is likely and the consequences are serious.

Activity 5   Deleting directories

Directories can be deleted in the same ways as files, so all the operations learnt in the previous activity apply equally to directories. Deleted directories, like files, cannot be undeleted. However you must take even more care as deleting a directory will delete any files and further subdirectories it contains (unlike MS-DOS). You must check the confirmation messages very carefully!

We will delete the TEST directory and the few remaining files it contains.

1.   If necessary make sure that the diskette containing the practice files is still inserted in A drive, open File Manager and check that the root directory a:\ is selected.

   Make sure that the TEST directory is selected, but none of its files.

   Open the **File** menu and select **Delete.**

   When the dialogue box appears only the directory name A:\TEST should be listed – see Figure 6 above.

   If a file name is selected then take the Cancel option, deselect the file (Ctrl key and click) and try again.

2.   Select the **OK** option and a further dialogue box appears – see Figure 8.

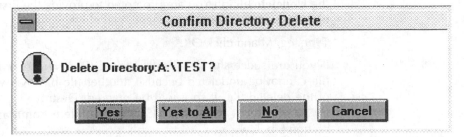

Figure 8

   Click the **Yes** option and you are prompted to confirm the deletion of each file in turn.

   Click Yes each time and the TEST directory and the files it conains are all deleted – check this in the directory tree.

3.   **Independent activity**

   Check that all our sample files have now been placed in the appropriate subdirectories. All files with SAL in the file name are now located in the SALES subdirectory, all files with ACC in the file name are located in the ACCOUNTS subdirectory.

   All files in the root directory A:\ are duplicates of these and can be deleted. Do this now.

Activity 6 Creating a system disk

Windows 3.1 and Windows for Workgroups need the MS-DOS operating system in order to run. MS-DOS consists of a number of files which are stored on the hard disk in the DOS directory. Certain of these system files are essential for your PC to start and to run. If they are accidentally removed, or damaged by a virus you will need a system disk to start or 'boot up' your computer.

Using File Manager you can transfer the key system files IO.SYS, MSDOS.SYS and COMMAND.COM to diskette. These three files will allow the system to re-start.

1. Take a spare formatted diskette and label it 'System Disk'.
    The diskette must not contain any files as they will be deleted.
    To add system files to an *un*formatted diskette you will need to use the Format Disk option on the Disk menu – see Unit 3, Activity 3.

2. Insert the diskette and call up File Manager if necessary.
    Change to A drive and check that the disk contains no files that you wish to keep.

3. Open the **Disk** menu and select the **Make system disk** option.
    A confirmation message appears. Check that the drive letter is correct and click the **Yes** button.

4. A copying message is displayed. This disappears once the system files are copied.
    If you get an error message check that the write protect notch on the diskette is closed

5. When File Manager is re-displayed only one file, COMMAND.COM is displayed. The other files are hidden in order to protect them.

    We will find out how to display them in Activity 7.

Activity 7 Displaying hidden files

Normally you can view all the files on disk using File Manager. However, some files are always hidden to protect them from interference, notably the key system files mentioned in the previous activity. It is essential that these files are not deleted or renamed, otherwise the computer will not run properly.

Sometimes it is useful to check that these hidden files are on your system disk.

1. Insert the system disk that you created in the last activity.

    Call up File Manager if necessary and change to A drive.

    Only one file is listed at the moment, COMMAND.COM; this is the command processor that executes certain key MS-DOS commands.

2. Open the **View** menu and select the **By File Type** option. A dialogue box appears.

   Click the 'Show Hidden/System Files' option.

   Click **OK.**

   Two more files are now displayed in File Manager – see Figure 9.

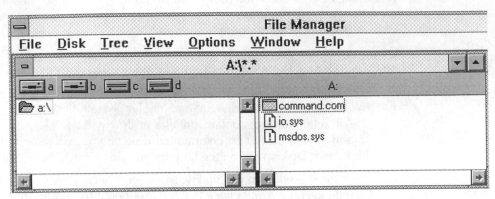

Figure 9

The ! sign on the icon identify them as files that are normally hidden, the .SYS extension identifies them as system files.

3. To find out their size and other details open the **View** menu and select the **All file details** option.

   The final column a lists the file attributes – r, h, s and a:

   r indicates read-only – the file is protected from amendment – it can be read but not written to,

   h indicates hidden – the file is not normally listed in File Manager,

   s indicates system file – it is part of the computer's operating system,

   a indicates archive – this attribute is used with certain MS-DOS copy commands to control whether a file is backed up.

4. Now we will hide these two files again.

   Open the **View** menu and select the **By File Type** option. A dialogue box appears.

   Click the 'Show System/Hidden Files' option to deselect it and remove the X sign from the box..

   Click **OK.**

   Only the COMMAND.COM file is now displayed in File Manager. IO.SYS and MSDOS.SYS are hidden again.

   A final warning. Do not list hidden files on a regular basis. They are hidden to prevent their being deleted, re-named or moved. It is all too easy to do this particularly if you are selecting blocks of files.

Similarly do not hide regular files – it is all too easy to forget where you have hidden them!

Activity 8 Independent activity

Your practice files are now stored in two directories – **SALES** and **ACCOUNTS.**

Create two further subdirectories in each directory called **MEMOS** and **LETTERS.**

Move all files with the word **LET** in their file names to subdirectory **LETTERS**

Move all files with the word **MEM** in their file names to the subdirectory **MEMOS.**

The final structure will be as follows:

```
SALES
    MEMOS
            MEMSAL1.TXT
            MEMSAL2.TXT
            MEMSAL3.TXT
            MEMSAL4.TXT
    LETTERS
            LETSAL1.WRI
            LETSAL2.WRI
            LETSAL3.WRI
            LETSAL4.WRI
ACCOUNTS
    MEMOS
            MEMACC1.TXT
            MEMACC2.TXT
            MEMACC3.TXT
            MEMACC4.TXT
    LETTERS
            LETACC1.WRI
            LETACC2.WRI
            LETACC3.WRI
            LETACC4.WRI
```

Summary of menu commands

Notes

Menu commands show the menu name first, followed by the command to choose from the menu, e.g. Edit-Clear means open the Edit menu and select the Clear command. Where a command is available from a particular window this is indicated in brackets.

(File Manager)

Disk – Make System Disk	Copy system files onto diskette
File – Associate	Associate a file with an application
File – Copy	Copy file
File – Create Directory	Create new directory
File – Delete	Delete a file or directory
File – Rename	Rename file or directory
View – By File Type	View different types of files

unit 8

Object linking and embedding

Introduction

More and more applications are Windows based – they use the features of the Windows graphical user interface (GUI for short). Once you have learned to use such features as the mouse, icons, windows, dialogue boxes and pull-down menus you can start to use any Windows application, eg a word processor, spreadsheet and database.

Users have also come to expect easy transfer of data between Windows applications; for example you may have created a graph using a spreadsheet and want to copy it into a word processed report. Also whenever the original graph changes you want the version in the report to be updated too – even though a word processor and a spreadsheet are completely different applications.

Microsoft (the producer of Windows) have created the standard for this to happen – OLE (pronounced 'oh lay' and short for Object Linking and Embedding)

Skills covered	Activity
Copying, cutting and painting	1
Embedding an object	1.6
Linking an object	2
Links – maintaining	3
Paintbrush – using	1

Previous skills required	Covered in unit
Using the standard Windows components	1
Opening, saving and minimising	
Windows applications	2

Resources required

Practice files created in Unit 2

95

Activity 1   Copying, pasting and embedding

1. **Copying and pasting**

   Open the **Paintbrush** application. It is part of the Accessories desktop.

   Produce the simple image shown in Figure 1: The exact shape and size do not matter, it is made up of an empty rounded box inside an empty box. Drawing them is simply a matter of clicking the shape to select the tool, then dragging on the Paintbrush screen to draw the shape – see Figure 2 if you have not used Paintbrush before.

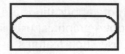

Figure 1

2. Select the image using the **Scissors** tool. (click the tool to select it, then drag to enclose the image)

   Open the **Edit** menu and select **Copy.**

3. Save the Paintbrush document on a diskette as IMAGE

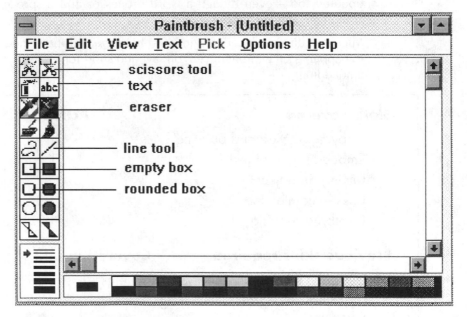

Figure 2

4. **Object embedding**

   Exit Paintbrush and open Windows **Write.**

   Type any few lines of text:

   Now open the **Edit** menu and select **Paste.** The image is pasted into the Write document.

5. Minimise the Write document and open the **Main** desktop.

   Open the **Clipboard viewer.** It contains the pasted image. Clipboard acts as the temporary storage area when data is cut or copied. It can only hold one chunk of data at a time, the next data to be copied or cut will overwrite the image.

6. Exit from the clipboard viewer and re-open the Write document.

   Click the image to select it. Now open the **Edit** menu and experiment with the **Move picture** and the **Size picture** options.

7. Try copying and cutting the image within the document, ie:

   select the image again,

   open the **Edit** menu and select **Cut** or **Copy,**

   locate the cursor where the image is to re-located,

   open the **Edit** menu and select **Paste.**

8. **In-place editing**

   If you need to edit the image you can change back to its 'home' application – Paintbrush – automatically

   Click the image to select it.

   Open the **Edit** menu and select **Edit paintbrush picture object** (or simply double-click the image)

   A Paintbrush window opens, allowing you to edit the image.

   Add a horizontal line to the image as shown in Figure 3 – use the line tool

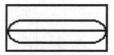

Figure 3

   Now open the **File** menu and select **Update.**

   Save the file as DOC1

   Open the **File** menu again and select **Exit**

   Return to the Write document and examine the image – it has been updated

   Now open the Paintbrush document IMAGE. The original image has not changed – there is no link between the two.

9. **Theory – read this next**

   Embedding

   What we have just done is to create information in a *'source'* document (Windows Paintbrush) and insert it into a *'destination'* document from a different application (Windows Write) This information – the image – became an *embedded* object. Any changes can be

97

made easily as an application window for the source application (Paintbrush) opens automatically from within the destination document (Write). When you embed an object in a document you **copy** the object from the source to the destination document. Once this happens the original and its copy cease to be linked in any way – editing the copy does not affect the original.

Activity 2 Object linking

Introduction

There are situations where you might want any changes to an original, eg a diagram or spreadsheet, to automatically update any copies of it that exist in other documents. In this case you can create a *link* to the original. (you can link several documents to one original)

Not all Windows applications are capable of supporting Object Linking. Of those that do some may be capable of acting as the source or *'server'* application; others may only be capable of acting as the destination or *'client'* application.

In the examples that follow we use Windows Paintbrush as the server Application and Windows Write as the client application.

1. Open a new Paintbrush document and create a simple map along the lines of Figure 4.

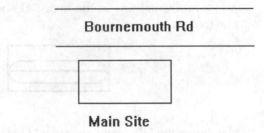

Bournemouth Rd

Main Site

Figure 4

2. Select the map using the **Scissors** tool.

    Select **Copy** from the **Edit** menu

3. Save the Paintbrush document onto diskette as MAP1

    Exit and close MAP1.

4. Open a new Write document and type the following text:

    'Below is a map showing the new site for the university building.'

    Leave a couple of blank lines.

    Open the **Edit** menu and select **Paste Link** (not Paste).

5. Save the Write document to diskette as DOC2 – the map is now linked to the original in the document MAP1

6. **Editing a linked drawing**

Double click on the map image, the Paintbrush document MAP1 containing the original map image is opened.

Arrange the Write window and the Paintbrush window so that the map image is visible in both documents. (drag the window using the title bar)

Amend the drawing by adding an IT Centre to the map as shown in Figure 5.

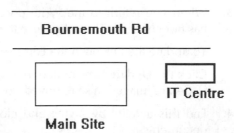

Figure 5

You will see both images are linked and change at the same time.

7. Open the **File** menu in the Paintbrush window and choose **Save**

Open the **File** menu in the Paintbrush window and choose **Exit.**

When you return to the Write document DOC2 the linked image has also changed.

Activity 3 Maintaining links

The links that we have established so far mean that any updates to linked objects are automatic, however you can make the links manual so that you can choose whether the linked object gets updated. You can also break or delete links and fix broken links, eg if the name of a linked document is changed.

At the moment the linked object in the Write document DOC2 is updated automatically.

We can change this default so that the update in optional.

1. Make sure that DOC2 is open

Open the **Edit** menu and select the **Links** option.

A dialogue box appears, showing the link to the Paintbrush document MAP1

Click the **Manual** button.

Click **OK.**

99

2. Now double click on the map image; the Paintbrush document MAP1 containing the original map image is opened as before.

   Arrange the Write window and the Paintbrush window as before, so that the map image is visible in both documents.

   Amend the Paintbrush image by removing the IT Centre from the map – use the Eraser tool. (see Figure 1 if necessary)

   Open the **File** menu in the Paintbrush window and choose **Save.**

   Open the **File** menu in the Paintbrush window and choose **Exit.**

3. When you return to the Write document DOC2 the linked image has not changed. This is because the link is now optional.

   To update the link open the **Edit** menu and select **Links.**

   Click the **Update Now** button then **OK –** the link is updated and the IT Centre image is also removed from the linked document.

4. End this activity by saving and closing the Write and Paintbrush documents.

5. **Amending the original document.** A linked object can be worked on in both the client and the server application. In the previous activity we edited the map image from within the client application, Windows Write. But we can just as easily do it from the server application, Windows Paintbrush. As the object is shared rather than copied then all linked client documents will change as well.

6. Open the Paintbrush document MAP1 and make a change to the map image.

   Save the changes and exit the document

   If the link is set to **manual** rather than **automatic** – see previous activity – then you will be prompted to update any linked documents. Do this now.

7. Now open the linked Write document DOC2 you will find that the map is updated.

   End this activity by closing all Write and Paintbrush documents.

Summary of menu commands

Notes

Menu commands show the menu name first, followed by the command to choose from the menu, e.g. Edit-Clear means open the Edit menu and select the Clear command. Where a command is available from a particular window this is indicated in brackets.

Edit – Copy	Copy selected section onto the Clipboard
Edit – Move/Size Picture	Move/Re-size selected picture within document
Edit – Links	Maintain links between linked documents
Edit – Paste	Insert copied section into document
Edit – Paste Link	Create link with the document from which the pasted element originates

101

Other Windows features

Introduction

This unit shows you how to package an object as an icon, how to check your system using Microsoft Diagnostics, and how to protect your system against viruses

Skills covered	Activity
Icons – packaging	1
Packaging an object	1
Hardware – checking	2
Memory – checking	2
Viruses – checking for	3

Previous skills required	Covered in unit
Using the standard Windows components	1
Opening, saving and minimising	
Windows applications	2

Resources required

The diskette containing the practice files created in Unit 2

Activity 1   Object packaging

Introduction

You now know how to link or embed information from one application in another – OLE. The Windows Object Packager allows you to represent a linked object as an icon. Clicking the icon calls up the object so it can be viewed or edited. This has many uses, eg, the user can call up additional text, such as a note, diagram or a definition, if he wants to refer to it. Windows Help uses this idea a lot, clicking on a keyword or icon displays further help text. You can also package an MS-DOS command as an icon so that it can be executed by clicking the icon. In the next activity we will create an icon that calls up MS-DOS help.

As with OLE, not every Windows application will necessarily support this feature.

1. Open the **Accessories** Group window

    Open **Object packager** – a Window is displayed

    Open the **Edit** menu and select **Command line** – a dialogue box is displayed.

2. Enter the MS-DOS command: **C:\DOS\HELP** (make sure that you use the colon and the back slash characters)

    Click the **OK** button – the command will now appear in the **Content** window – see Figure 1.

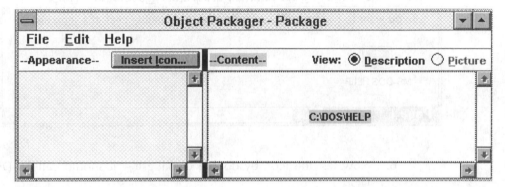

Figure 1

3. Now click the **Insert** Icon button – a group of icons appears

    Select a suitable one to represent your MS-DOS command.

    Click **OK** – it is shown in the **Appearance** window.

4. Open the **Edit** menu and select **Label**

    Enter the label 'MS-DOS Help' in the dialogue box and click **OK**

    The icon is now labelled – see Figure 2.

5. Open the **Edit** menu and select **Copy Package** (not Copy).

    Now open a new **Windows Write** document and type the text;

    'If you want to call up MS-DOS help now, double click the icon below'

    Now open the **Edit** menu and select **Paste.** The icon appears – see Figure 3.

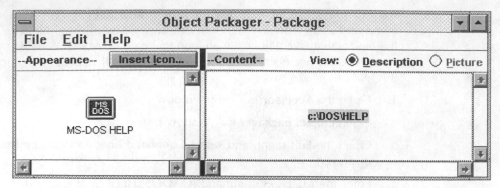

Figure 2

Figure 3

6. Now test the icon by double clicking it – it should call up DOS Help

   When you exit Help you will be returned to the Write document.

   Save the document to diskette as HELP_TXT

7. **Note:** The icon can be edited if necessary by selecting it, then choosing Package Object – Edit Object from the Edit menu.

Activity 2   Checking your hardware

Introduction

Windows offers Microsoft Diagnostics (MSD) which provides technical information about all aspects of your system, including the hardware. Some are too technical for a publication of this type but others can be used to provide useful supplementary information such as the type of central processing unit, hard disk types and memory.

1. Open File Manager. Select C drive then the Windows directory.

   Locate the MSD.EXE program file and double click to run – this file will normally be located in the Windows directory rather than one of its subdirectories.

The Microsoft Diagnostics main menu screen appears, showing a general description of your computer – memory, disk drives, monitor attached (video) etc.

2. Each of the grey boxes can be selected to provide more detailed information. (use the mouse or type the highlighted letter) Try this for some of the options.

3. At the top of the screen are 3 menus – File, Utilities and Help.

   Select the **File** menu using the mouse or the Alt key. A number of key system files are listed. Two of them, AUTOEXEC.BAT, CONFIG.SYS etc are discussed in more detail in the units on MS-DOS.

4. **Independent activity.** Use MSD to find out:
   a. free space on your main disk drive.
   b. your Windows version.
   c. your processor type.
   Exit MSD.

Activity 3 Checking for viruses (Windows for Workgroups only)

Introduction

The first computer viruses appeared on PC's in the 1980's. There are now several thousand viruses in circulation. They can spread, often unnoticed, and pose a serious threat to any computer system. Organisations have been compelled to establish anti-virus measures to combat the threat. A computer virus is a small program that spreads by attaching itself to another program on disk. The infected program may attack a COM or EXE file, or the boot sector of the disk. (this stores instructions so that the operating system can start to read or 'boot' the disk)
When the infected program is run the virus looks for other programs to infect.
Despite scare stories in the media most viruses are merely nuisances, displaying strange messages or making the system behave oddly. Some however can corrupt or destroy data by eg, formatting disks or deleting files. Viruses are usually spread through organisations by using an infected diskette brought from home or another infected site. Many businesses and colleges now forbid the use of diskettes brought from outside, because of the high cost of removing even a relatively harmless virus.
Virus checking software has the almost impossible task of recognising the new viruses and variants that are emerging all the time. The most common method is to scan the suspect disk for *recognition strings* – a series of bytes that occur in known viruses, but not in a harmless program. Another detection method is the checksum. This performs a mathematical calculation based on the bytes of data in each file and

stores the result. A virus will modify the size of the file it infects and the *checksum* will detect this if run again.

You usually have the options to schedule automatic virus scans at regular intervals or to have the the program permanently running in the background – this saves you having to remember to run the anti-virus program.

Windows provides the Microsoft Antivirus program MWAV. Your version may well be out of date unless you subscribe to the update service and will not be as comprehensive as market leaders such as Norton or Dr Solomons. We will use it to try out some of the anti-virus features.

1. Open the **Main** group window and double click the MWAV icon.

   Insert practice disk a in the machine and select the appropriate diskette drive letter.

   MWAV reads the disk and shows disk, directory and file information in the Status window.

2. Click the **Detect** button. All the files in all directories of the current disk are scanned. When complete a report is displayed, showing the number and type of files scanned.
   If your disk is free of viruses then columns 2 and 3 should show no infected files.

   Click the **OK** button.

3. Now select your hard drive and take the Detect option again to scan the hard disk for viruses.

4. Open the **Scan** menu and take the **Virus list** option. A list of all the viruses recognised by MWAV is displayed. Use the scroll bar or the PgDn key to scroll through it.

   Find out more about some of the viruses – select the name and then the **Info** button.

   Click **OK** to return to the Main Menu.

5. **Independent activity.** Use the Help option to find out about stealth viruses and checksums on the Options menu.

6. Exit from MWAV.

Summary of menu commands

Notes

Menu commands show the menu name first, followed by the command to choose from the menu, e.g. Edit-Clear means open the Edit menu and select the Clear command. Where a command is available from a particular window this is indicated in brackets.

(Object Packager)

Edit – Command Line	Create a packaged MS-DOS command
Edit – Label	Label an icon
Edit – Copy Package	Copy packaged object

Part 2

MS-DOS

Introduction

Why learn MS-DOS?

As explained in the Preface, Windows is now more popular than MS-DOS. Windows 95 does not require MS-DOS in order to run, unlike previous versions of Windows, so this trend will accelerate. However there are still millions of PC users using applications written for MS-DOS rather than Windows. Even if you only use Windows applications it can still be a good idea to learn MS-DOS:

❐ there are certain Windows commands that are still based around MS-DOS. For example you can use the MS-DOS 'wildcard' command to, copy or delete all files with similar names.

❐ Some MS-DOS commands are easier than their Windows equivalents – or they have no Windows equivalent. For example you can use the UNDELETE command, to reverse a DELETE command, and the UNFORMAT command to reverse the effects of an unwanted disk formatting.

❐ Learning MS-DOS and its structure will give you a good insight into how a computer operates. The Windows interface tends to hide much of this from the casual user behind icons and menus.

❐ Learning MS-DOS is valuable in helping you to deal with common problems in managing your disks and files.

This section does not encourage casual experimentation with vital PC settings and configuration, eg fine tuning the main memory and disk caching. Later versions of MS-DOS and Windows have increasingly automated these tricky areas, where the untrained user can cause havoc to the way the PC runs!

What is an Operating System?

The operating system is a special set of programs that controls the basic operations of a PC, in particular controlling the flow of data between the its various parts, eg sending data from the keyboard, controlling the screen display and transferring data between the main memory and the disk drives. When you, eg, call up a program the operating system locates it on disk, retrieves it and stores it in main memory so that you can use it. It acts as an invisible bridge between the hardware – the physical parts of the computer – and the software – the various programs running on it.

As well as these invisible tasks the user can use MS-DOS to perform housekeeping tasks like listing, copying and deleting files and formatting disks. (MS-DOS version 6 includes extra utilities such as a virus checker, and a disk compressor that can double available disk space)

A more elaborate definition of an operating system will only confuse you at this stage if you are new to PC's. You will learn a lot more when you have worked your way through these activities.

A note on drives

The hard disk, usually designated drive C, is used to store MS-DOS, Windows, and other applications, e.g. word processor, spreadsheet or database. If you have enough disk space you can also use C drive to save work that you create. However it is common to save work on a diskette (also known as a floppy disk) especially where space on the hard disk is limited or if you want to work on more than one computer.

In the activities in these units we shall be using diskettes to save work. The diskette drive is referred to as A drive.

Diskettes needed

For the MS-DOS activities you will need two suitable three and a half inch high density diskettes, (floppy disks) preferably new ones that do not contain any files. The Format and Delete commands will erase any information on them. If you have completed the Windows exercises for Part 1 these disks can be re-used.

A brand new disk needs to be formatted before it can be used – consult Unit 1 Activity 5 for information on different disk formats if necessary.

Conventions used in Part 2

The terms 'DOS' and 'MS-DOS' are used interchangeably.

The terms 'PC', 'personal computer' and 'computer' are used interchangeably.

Commands may be typed in lower or upper case. I use upper case for clarity. If you wish to use upper case then use the Caps Lock key.

Every command has to be followed by pressing the **Enter** key. This sends the command to the computer's processing unit. I shan't be reminding you of this after the first few activities.

Unless otherwise stated an activity will work with all versions of MS-DOS from version 5 onwards.

unit 10
MS-DOS – the introductory essentials

Introduction

In this unit you will learn such essential preliminaries as starting MS-DOS, setting the date and time, changing drives, formatting a disk and listing files.

Skills Covered	Activity
Help – getting	2
Date – checking	4
Directory commands – using	7
Disk drive – changing	6
Diskette – formatting	5
File types – identifying	7
Files – listing	7
MS-DOS Version – checking	3
System disk – creating	5.2
Time – checking	4

Previous skills required

None

Activity 1   Starting MS-DOS

Although MS-DOS is automatically loaded when the PC is turned on, your PC may have been set up to start Windows or display a menu straight afterwards. If so it is a matter of exiting and returning to MS-DOS.

1.   Turn on the PC (and the screen too if necessary)
     Various system checks are made and various messages will be
     displayed briefly on the screen.
     Look out for any messages about the BIOS – Basic Input Output
     System. This is the first part of the operating system and is perma-
     nently installed in your PC on a special component – the ROM
     BIOS microprocessor or 'chip'. ROM stand for Read Only Memory,
     meaning that the manufacturer's instructions on the chip cannot be
     altered ('written to'), only 'read' or carried out. Apart from a few
     settings which you should *not* interfere with, you cannot control
     this part of the system. The BIOS (Basic Input and Output System)
     controls the basic operations of the computer input and output
     devices such as disk drives and keyboards.

     After checking these the BIOS loads the main part of the operating
     system – MSDOS – which is stored on the hard disk. It searches for
     certain key files, including the main command processor
     COMMAND.COM and two other vital files CONFIG.SYS and
     AUTOEXEC.BAT. We will be finding out more about them in later
     activities.

2.   After your PC has finished booting up (the name given to the above
     start-up operations) – check the screen

     If you can see the symbol C:\> or similar then you are in MS-DOS.
     Go on to section 3.

     If not try the following:

     a.   If you see the Windows logo followed by the the Windows
          screen you will need to exit from Windows.
          Look for the Word 'File' at the top left of the Windows screen.
          Move the mouse so that the screen pointer is located on top of
          the word 'File' and click the left mouse button once.
          The File menu opens, showing a number of options, take the
          Exit or Exit Windows option.
          You may be asked to confirm this, if so use the mouse to click
          the Yes or OK button.

          You may have to go back several Windows screens to finally
          leave Windows. When you can see the symbol C:\> or
          similar then you are in MS-DOS. Go on to section 3.

     b.   If your PC is displaying a menu or set of choices look for the
          Exit option – perhaps it is labelled 'Quit Menus' or 'Exit to
          DOS'. You may have to return to a main menu before you can
          do this.

          Follow the directions on the menu, eg type the option number
          and press the Enter key. This large L-shaped key is on the right
          of the keyboard and marked with a curled arrow.

3.   **The MS-DOS prompt.** Your PC should now be displaying a system
     prompt such as C:\>,D:\> or A:\> . The first letter indicates which
     drive is currently in use – the 'active' drive.

111

C and **D** refer to hard disk drives

A normally refers to the diskette or floppy disk drive, if you have a second diskette drive then this will be B drive.

F normally indicates that your computer is connected to a local area network.

The next part of the prompt consists of the symbol \> or similar. The backslash (\) symbol indicates that you are in the main or root directory of the disk – a concept that we shall be looking at in detail later – see Unit 11, Activity 1.

If you have just left Windows or a menu system you may not be in the root directory, in which case try the following, otherwise go on to Activity 2.

Notes: Does your MS-DOS prompt read C:\WINDOWS> or C:\MENU> or similar?

If so type the command CD \ and press the Enter key. You will be returned to the root directory.

If you have no diskette drive, or are connected to a local area network then you will need to seek further advice before you carry on with these activities.

Activity 2 Getting help

Now that we have started MS-DOS we can try out our first command – HELP. This can be a valuable source of reference in finding out what commands are available and how to use them.

1. Type the command **HELP** (upper or lower case) then press the **Enter** key. A list of DOS commands is displayed with a short description of each.

    MS-DOS 5 Press **Enter** to go on to the next screen. Eventually the MS-DOS prompt is displayed again.

    MS-DOS 6 on. A list of contents is displayed. To select more detailed information you can use the mouse or the keyboard.
    Either use the mouse to move the screen pointer onto the required command and click, or type the initial letter of the command.

2. Exit Help and return to the MS-DOS prompt.

3. If you know the command name and want further help with it then merely type HELP followed by the command itself.

    Type the command **HELP VER** and press the Enter key. A brief explanation of the **VER** command follows.

4. Exit Help and type the command **HELP HELP** and press the Enter key. A brief explanation of the HELP command follows.
Exit Help again.

Activity 3   Checking the MS-DOS version

Microsoft have released many versions of DOS over the years. You will need to know which version is installed on your PC when you are using these units. The version is also important when you are acquiring software for your PC; sometimes later versions of software need later versions of MS-DOS to run properly.

1. The command to check the MS-DOS version is simply VER.

   Type the command **VER** and press the Enter key. The version of MS-DOS is displayed. If it is MS-DOS 5 or later then these units are for you. If it is an earlier version of MS-DOS then some of the MS-DOS activities in these units may not work.

Activity 4   Setting the date and time

All PC's have a battery-powered internal clock. DOS uses this clock to record the date and time that a file is created or changed. When you list your files the date and time are listed next to the file name – see Activity 7. This helps you to keep track of your files, eg to find the latest version of a file. Sometimes this clock requires to be reset.

1. Type the command **DATE** and press Enter.

   The current system date is displayed, eg,

   > Current Date is Wed 06-12-1995

   > Enter new date (dd-mm-yy)

   This simple command and response is the basis of most MS-DOS processing:

   a. Data is input via the keyboard

   b. The Enter key sends this input to be processed.

   c. The operating system outputs its response to the screen

2. Press the Enter key to accept the date shown

3. Issue the DATE command again. This time type in the date of your next birthday – you must use the format exactly as shown – three sets of digits, separated by the – dash symbol, eg 08-03-1996

   Press Enter.

4. Notice that no confirmation of a successful command is given – this is common in DOS! If you mis-typed the date an invalid date message will be displayed and you can try again.

113

5. Issue the DATE command again – you can see the day on which your birthday falls! Now reset the date to the correct one. If you don't do this then any file creations or amendments will be wrongly dated.

6. **Note.** Your PC may prompt you for the date in US format, ie month-day-year. If so you will need to type the date as prompted, eg 12-21-1995

7. **Independent activity. Setting the time.**

    Issue the TIME command (plus Enter) to check the system time. The time is displayed in hours, minutes, seconds, and hundredths of a seconds, each separated with a colon (a 'p' or 'a' may indicate pm or am)

    To reset the time you only need to enter the hours and minutes, using the 24 hour clock format.

    Set the Time to 19:57 and type TIME again to check it.

    Re-set the clock to the correct time when you have finished.

Activity 5   Formatting a diskette

Introduction

A new diskette is normally sold unformatted; it cannot be used until it has been formatted. To practise this activity you will need a diskette, preferably new and unused. Formatting divides the diskette into electro-magnetic tracks so that information can be stored on it. It also creates an empty directory that will be used to find the files on the disk.
If you format a used disk any information already stored on it will be erased, however the UNFORMAT command provided by MS-DOS can restore the information.

Recognising high density disks

All new PC's use the standard three and a half inch, high density 1.44 Mb diskettes. Don't use the older double density 720kb disks for this activity.

How many square holes does your disk have? All disks have one – the write protect notch which can be opened to protect the files from being changed. Only high density disks have a second hole – this is your best guide, though some manufacturers stamp 'HD' on their disks.

1. Now type the command **FORMAT A:** and press the Enter key.

    MS-DOS prompts you:

    > Insert new diskette for drive A:
    >
    > and press ENTER when ready...

114

Insert the diskette in A drive – silver clip first and embossed arrow on top pointing forward.

The disk format is checked, then formatting – a slow process – begins. The disk is divided into 80 *tracks* on both sides of the disk. Concentric tracks on different disk surfaces are called *cylinders*.

When formatting is 100% complete you are prompted:

Volume label (11 characters, ENTER for none)?

You may give the disk a name or label; this can be a useful identifier. Enter a suitable label, eg DOS_FILES and press Enter.

MS-DOS displays the capacity of the disk in bytes, eg:

1457664 bytes total disk space

1457664 bytes available on disk

A byte holds one character, eg a letter or number, 1K or a kilobyte holds just over 1,000 characters (1024 in fact), 1MB or a megabyte just over a million characters.
The total disk space is slightly more than 1.44MB. Sometimes the bytes available are less than the total disk space due to bad sectors on the disk. This is quite usual and nothing to worry about providing the difference is not greater than 64K.

Finally DOS asks you:

Format another (Y/N)?

If you wish to format another disk at this stage type **Y** (plus Enter), otherwise type **N** and press Enter.

2. **Creating a system disk**

When your PC starts up it does so using system files stored on C drive – see Activity 1. If these files should be damaged you would be unable to start the computer and thus could not replace them. For this reason it is wise to create a system or boot disk so that the PC can be restarted. This can be done by adding the /S switch to the format command.

Make sure that your diskette is still in A drive, then issue the command, **FORMAT A: /S** and proceed as before.
Eventually DOS confirms with the message 'System transferred'. The disk is formatted again as a system disk. Normally, of course, you would not format the same disk twice.

Activity 6   Changing drives

Introduction – concepts and terminology

a.   **Disk drives.**

Your computer probably has at least two drives, the diskette drive, known as A drive, and the hard disk, known as C drive. You may well have other drives or be connected to a network or have a CD-ROM drive.

Whenever you refer to a drive you do so using the letter followed by a colon symbol, e.g. A: or C: (upper or lower case)

The diskette drive is usually used to store data in a portable form (ie on diskettes or floppy disks that can be removed) The hard disk is permanently fixed in the machine and holds MS-DOS, Windows and other applications, e.g. spreadsheet, word processor or database. It can also be used to store data. As the hard disk and its drive are one unit it can be referred to as either hard disk or hard drive.

b.   **Files.**

Whatever you create on a computer has to be saved as a named file. When you save a file you are copying information from the computer's main memory (RAM), which is temporary, to a permanent site on disk. If you did not save your work in this way it would be lost when the computer was turned off. A file on a computer is therefore similar to a paper file in a filing cabinet. Both need a file name to file them away and retrieve them.

1.   **Changing drives.** Changing drives is simply a matter of typing the drive letter followed by a colon, eg A: or C:

Look at the DOS prompt on screen.

If it is displaying **C:\>** then this means that,

C: the hard disk is the active drive

\ the root or main directory is the current directory (see Activity 8)

> indicates that DOS is prompting you for a command.

Only one drive and directory can be active at one time.

If the C:\> prompt is not displayed type **C:** and press Enter.

If any other name follows the \ symbol then type the command **CD ** and press Enter. This will return you to the root directory.

Troubleshooting:

If you get the messages 'Invalid Drive Specification' or 'Bad command or file name' then you may have typed the commands incorrectly. Common errors are typing a semicolon instead of a colon and typing a forward slash (/) instead of the back slash (\).

The 'Invalid Drive Specification' message may mean that your PC has no hard drive, particularly if you are connected to a network. If so seek advice.

2. Make sure that the disk that you formatted in the last activity is in A drive.

    Type the command **A:** and press Enter.

    The prompt A:\> should now be displayed. This means that A: the diskette drive is now the active drive.

3. **Common errors**

    Try these next:

    Type the command A; The use of the semicolon instead of the colon causes the command to be rejected. After the error message the A:\> waits for your next command for your next command.

    Remove the diskette from A drive then type the command A:

    The error message appears:

    'Not ready error reading drive A

    Abort, Retry, Fail?'

    You have tried to activate an empty disk drive.

    Insert the disk and press **R** to retry.

    The A:\> prompt is displayed again.

Activity 7   Listing files

Introduction

A diskette can store dozens of files, a hard disk can store hundreds. To make files easier to locate they are placed into separate groups or directories – like drawers in a filing cabinet. In this Activity we'll be finding out how list them, using the DIR command. Short for directory, it lists the files on your disk or in a directory. In Unit 11 we'll be learning more complex tasks, such as sorting them into different orders.

1. If necessary change to C drive. (type C: plus Enter)

    Issue the DIR command again. All the files and directories on your hard disk are displayed. On my hard disk they appear as follows, but the directory listing will obviously vary from PC to PC.

117

```
Volume in drive C is C DRIVE
Volume Serial Number is 1D88-9BA0
Directory of C:\

DOS                  <DIR>              08/12/94   19:29
CONFIG      OLD                  254   11/12/94   11:25
AUTOEXEC    BAT                  282   04/12/94   22:03
COMMAND     COM               54,645   31/05/94    6:22
WINDOWS              <DIR>              08/12/94   20:01
CONFIG SYS                      268   14/12/94   22:03
TEMP2                <DIR>              08/12/94   19:54

7 file(s)  55,449 bytes
6,842,368 bytes free
```

Find the two subdirectories named DOS and WINDOWS (directories are shown in pointed brackets) These two subdirectories store the files that you need to run Windows and MS-DOS.

Rules for filenames. In MS-DOS and Windows a file name can consist of up to 8 characters, these can be the letters A to Z (upper or lower case) or numbers 0 to 9.

Certain other keyboard characters can be used, including the dash (-), and the underscore character (_).

The following *cannot* be used: space, comma, full stop, slash, colon, semicolon, brackets, quotation marks and the equals sign.

The file name is usually followed by an *extension* of up to three characters, separated from the file name by a full stop or 'dot'.

The extension usually identifies the type of file, and is often automatically allocated by the program which creates it. It is useful to recognise the types of file in a directory listing.

The following file extensions are common:

.COM is a short program or command file.

.EXE files are also program files – double clicking them executes or runs them.

.HLP files contain the help text for various applications, eg the help text for a DOS command.

.TXT files are text files. They contain only the basic keyboard characters a to z and 0 to 9, plus puctuation marks and other typable keyboard characters.

Text files are also referred to as ASCII files (American Standard Code for Information Interchange), indicating that they contain only the standard characters. In addition to creating simple notes and memos it can be used to create and edit batch files – see Unit 16. You will also come across notepad files with the extension .DOC or named READ.ME which usually contain information about an application.

.WRI and .WP files are text files created in a word processor. Unlike .TXT files they contain many special (usually invisible) characters that control the appearance and layout of the text, e.g. bold, font size, line spacing, columns. These are essential to create more complex documents, but vary between different word processors.

.SYS files are system files that contol part of the computer hardware, like keyboard or printer.

.BAT files are batch program files. They are used to store a batch of MS-DOS commands which can be run when required – see Unit 16, Activity 2.

2. **Directory information.** The DIR command provides essential information about each file in 6 columns. Identify the following columns in your directory listing:

    Columns 1 and 2 – file\directory name and optional extension

    Column 3 – identifies directories

    Column 4 – file size in bytes (see Activity 5)

    Columns 5 and 6 – date and time of creation/amendment

    Notice that the DIR command also lists the number of files. The remaining free disk space is also displayed, in the listing above about 6.8 Megabytes.

    The names with extensions are files, eg AUTOEXEC.BAT, the names in brackets are further directories (subdirectories), eg DOS, WINDOWS. These directories, as we shall see, contain further files and/or directories.

3. **Using the DIR command with switches.** Often the directory listing is too long and the file names scroll off the screen. To prevent this we add the the 'pause' switch.

    Type **DIR /P** (plus Enter)
    The directory is listed a screenful at a time.
    Press any key to see the next screen (if any).

    Now type **DIR /W** (plus Enter)
    The directory is listed in wide format – but note that much of the information gets omitted.

    These are two examples of how a basic command can be refined by adding switches

4. **Exercises.** Use the DIR/P command and note down:
    ❐   Which is the largest file listed?
    ❐   Which file was created first?
    ❐   Which different file extensions are used?

5. **Paper exercise only.** Look at the following file names and write down which ones are invalid and why.

(Answers given in Appendix 2)

- ❐ BUDGET.1
- ❐ JUNEBUDGET.1..vvv
- ❐ ACCN_MAY
- ❐ ACCN\MAY.WRK
- ❐ MEMBERS.DBF1
- ❐ MEMBERS.DBF
- ❐ APR SLS.XLS

Warning – From Now on.....

I shall not be reminding you of the need to press the Enter key to execute a command!

Summary of commands

Notes:

Optional elements of commands are shown in square brackets [ ]

Do **not** include these square brackets when you type the command, they are only there to guide you.

Commands may be typed in uppercase or lowercase.

All commands must be followed by pressing the Enter Key

DATE	Display/Change the system date
DIR	Show files/subdirectories in current directory
DIR [drive:][directory name]	Show files/subdirectories in named directory
DIR/P	Show files/subdirectories, pausing every screenful
DIR/W	Show files/subdirectories in wide display
DIR>PRN	Send directory listing to printer
FORMAT drive:[/S][/Q]	Format disk in named drive, eg FORMAT A: /Sadds system files, /Q performs quick format
HELP	Call up MS-DOS help
HELP[command]	Get help on named command
TIME	Display/Change the system time
VER	Display MS-DOS version

Files and directories

Introduction

In this Unit you will learn how to about directories – the structure of directories and subdirectories and how to change from one to another. You will find out how to sort and locate files in different ways. We will also look at the structure of MS-DOS commands.

Skills covered	Activity
Control-menu box – using	2.2
Commands – understanding	3
Directory – changing	1
Directory Tree – displaying	2
Directory Tree – printing	2.6
Doskey – installing	5.6
File Attributes – displaying	6
Files – searching multiple directories	5.8
Files – showing	1, 5
Files – sorting	4
Previous command – recalling	5.5
System prompt – showing	1.2
Wild card searching	5

Previous skills required

How to start MS-DOS – see Unit 10, Activity 1

Activity 1   Changing directories

Introduction

So far you have only listed the files in the root directory. The root or main directory is usually divided into further subdirectories. A typical structure might be as Figure 1:

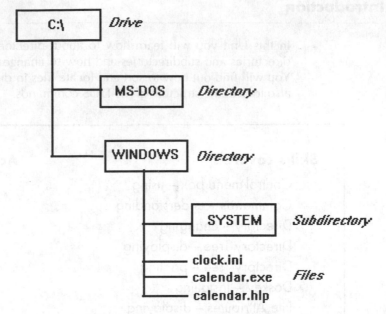

Figure 1

This shows the inverted tree structure used by MS-DOS and Windows. The root directory is at the top (represented by '\' the backslash character) and can be divided, like branches on a tree, into further directories, each of which in their turn can be divided into further subdirectories. So each directory holds a collection of files and/or further (sub)directories. The CD command allows you to change directories.

1.   Make sure that C is the active drive (type C: if not)

Type the command **CD \WINDOWS** (the space between the CD and the \ character is optional)
DOS takes you down one directory level to the WINDOWS subdirectory.

The DOS prompt should now read C:\WINDOWS> as most PC's are set up to show the current directory within the prompt. This confirms that you are in the WINDOWS subdirectory of the root directory on C drive.

2. **Troubleshooting – checking the system prompt.**

   a. If you get the message 'Invalid directory' check the command again, especially spelling and the backslash.

   b. If only the C prompt is shown type CD (on its own CD tells you which directory you are in)

   If DOS confirms C:\WINDOWS then you have changed to this directory successfully. You will need to reset the prompt so that it displays the current directory.

   Type the command **PROMPT PG**

   DOS now displays the current directory path – you will need to remember to type this command every time you start a new DOS session for the activities that follow. Alternatively the PROMPT PG command can be included in the AUTOEXEC.BAT file to make it a permanent setting – see Unit 15, Activity 5.

3. Type the DIR command. All the files and directories in the WINDOWS directory are displayed. It stores all the files that you need to run Windows.

4. Type the DIR /W and DIR /P commands and study the screen displays.

   Next type the TREE command.
   You will find that the Windows directory contains several further subdirectories as well as files. Depending how your system has been set up; you will have at least one, SYSTEM

5. Let's go down another directory level and change to one of these subdirectories.

   Type the command **CD SYSTEM** – the DOS prompt should now read C:\WINDOWS\SYSTEM> – confirming you are in the SYSTEMS subdirectory of the WINDOWS directory in the root directory of C drive. (the backslash ' \ ' symbol not only denotes the root directory but is used to separate levels of subdirectory)

   Type **DIR /P** to display the contents of the directory.

   It contains no further subdirectories, but over 100 files

   You have gone down two directory levels in all –

   The root (\) directory contains the WINDOWS directory
   The WINDOWS directory contains the SYSTEM subdirectory

   Diagrammatically it looks like Figure 2.

6. **Going up one directory level**

   Type **CD..** (ie CD followed by two full stops)

   The DOS prompt should now read C:\WINDOWS> you have left the SYSTEM subdirectory and returned to its 'parent' directory WINDOWS

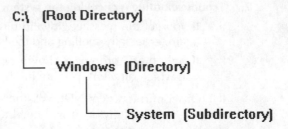

C:\ [Root Directory]

Windows [Directory]

System [Subdirectory]

Figure 2

7. **Returning to the root directory**

The command CD \ will return you to the root directory, whatever level of subdirectory you are in.

First type the command **CD SYSTEM** to return to the SYSTEM subdirectory – the DOS prompt will now read C:\WINDOWS\SYSTEM> again.

Now type CD \ and you are returned to the root directory.

8. Moving across a directory level. Look at the following DOS tree diagram shown in Figure 3,

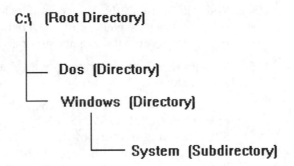

C:\ [Root Directory]

Dos [Directory]

Windows [Directory]

System [Subdirectory]

Figure 3

DOS and the WINDOWS are both directories in the root directory.

Change to the WINDOWS directory again – the DOS prompt will now read C:\WINDOWS>

Now try changing to the DOS directory by typing the command:

CD DOS

You will get the message 'Invalid directory'. This is because you have not given the full command. The DOS directory is not in the WINDOWS directory but in the root directory, so you need to give the full 'path' to the directory – the route through the other directories to reach the one that you want.

Type the command **CD \DOS** and you will be successful – the DOS prompt should now read C:\DOS>

124

9. Finally let's try moving across to the WINDOWS directory then down to its 'child' subdirectory SYSTEM in one command.

   Type **CD \WINDOWS\SYSTEM**

   The DOS prompt should now read C:\WINDOWS\SYSTEM> – confirming you are in the SYSTEMS subdirectory of the WINDOWS directory

Activity 2   Displaying the directory tree

Introduction

As we have discovered in previous activities a disk has a root or main directory, which is usually divided into further subdirectories. A typical structure might be as Figure 4:

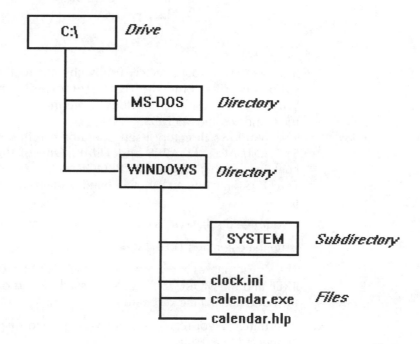

Figure 4

This shows the inverted tree structure adopted by MS-DOS and Windows with the root directory at the top (represented by '\' the back-slash character) divided like branches on a tree into further directories and subdirectories. each of these subdirectories can in their turn can be divided into further subdirectories. So each directory holds a collection of files and/or further directories.

1. Make sure that C is the active drive – if the C:\> prompt is not displayed type C: to change to C drive and then **CD** to change to the root directory.

125

You are now in the root directory on C drive (designated by the \ symbol in the DOS prompt)

2. Type the command **TREE** and press Enter.
The TREE command displays a diagram of all the directories and subdirectories on disk. The tree diagram for C drive is listed vertically, Figure 5 shows the one for the C drive on my PC. (your diagram may differ from this)

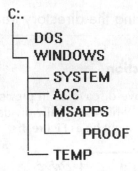

Figure 5

It shows C:\ the root directory first, within the root are a number of subdirectories. Find the two directories named DOS and WINDOWS. These two directories store the files that you need to run Windows and MS-DOS.
The Windows directory itself contains 4 futher subdirectories, SYSTEM. ACC, MSAPPS and TEMP. One of these, MSAPPS, contains a further subdirectory PROOF.
The DOS directory, on the other hand contains no further subdirectories.

3. If your tree display scrolls off the screen you can pause it.

Issue the command **TREE | MORE**

The screen pauses every screenful. (the 'pipe' symbol between the TREE and the MORE commands is usually found on the '\' key to the bottom left of the keyboard)

4. Alternatively you can print out your screen display if you are connected to a printer.

Issue the command **TREE>PRN**

The '>' symbol redirects the output of the TREE command to the printer rather than the screen. 'PRN' is the standard DOS name for a printer.

If you are connected to a network then you may have to seek further advice.

Troubleshooting. If you get strings of characters rather than lines joining the directories on your printout then you will need to add a switch to the TREE command.

126

Type **HELP TREE**

You will see that there are two switches explained:

The /A switch uses ASCII characters instead of extended characters, i.e. it represents the lines of the directory tree by a series of codes that the printer can interpret correctly.

Exit Help.

In this case type **TREE/A>PRN**

(nb the forward slash is used for switches – don't confuse it with the backslash that you have been using for directories)

5. **Displaying the files in each directory**

Type **HELP TREE** again. You will see that the /F switch is used to display the names of the files in each directory.

Exit Help.

Type **TREE/F**

All the files in all directories are displayed – far too many to fit on the screen.

Type **TREE/F I MORE** The screen pauses at every screen – but there are still too many files and directories to scan easily.

6. If you have a printer then instead of the IMORE command you can use the TREE command to print the contents of the WINDOWS directory and the directories and files that they contain.

Type the command **TREE/A/F C:\WINDOWS>PRN**

If you get an error message then check the command very carefully, in particular the forward (/) and back (\) slashes, the colon (:) and the redirection sign (>)

Activity 3 Understanding the structure of MS-DOS commands

Introduction

If you are new to DOS and have struggled through the last command – TREE/A/F C:\WINDOWS>PRN – you may rightly feel that DOS command structure is complex and 'fiddly'. When DOS was originally launched in 1981 it was not intended for the beginner or occasional user. It has been improved since then but not very much; Windows has filled the need for a user-friendly interface rather than DOS. However the structure of DOS is relatively simple once you have learnt a few rules, and can often be quicker and more powerful than navigating the icons, menus and dialogue boxes in Windows. The structure of DOS is known as its syntax. Unless you follow the syntax or grammatical rules the commands will not work.

1. **Basic command syntax**

   A command consists of up to three parts;

   the *command name* eg DIR, CD or TREE *parameters* which identify the object the command is to operate on, eg the directory name

   switches which modify how the command works, eg the switches /W and /P modify how the DIR command works.

2. Type **HELP TREE**

   After the explanation of the command the formal command syntax is given –

   TREE [drive:][path] [/F] [/A]

   It's important that you understand this syntax otherwise you will be unable to look up commands and type them correctly:

   A command consists of several elements, some of which may be optional. Optional elements are shown in square brackets [ ]
   Do **not** include these square brackets when you type the command, they are only there to guide you.

   Commands may be typed in uppercase or lowercase.

3. Now look at the labelled version of the TREE command below in Figure 6.

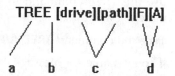

Figure 6

   a. is the command name itself, this *must* always be included. In the case of the TREE command everything else is optional. TREE on its own will display the directory tree for the current drive and directory, ie the one that you happen to be using when you issue the command.

   b. A single space should separate the command name from the rest of the command. Omitting it is a common source of error.

   c. Drive and Path is a very common parameter; it tells DOS the route that it must take to locate the files that you want to work with – these files may be on another drive and in another directory to the one you are currently in.

   d. Switches modify the way a command operates, we have already used these two switches for the TREE command in the previous activity.

4. Look at the following directory tree in Figure 7;

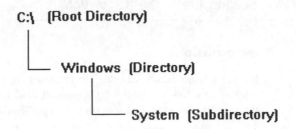

C:\ [Root Directory]

Windows [Directory]

System [Subdirectory]

Figure 7

If we are in the root or main directory and we want to use the TREE command to show the files in a subdirectory then we have to describe to MS-DOS how to find them – the 'path' to them.
So to display the tree diagram for the WINDOWS subdirectory the command is

TREE \WINDOWS

To display the tree diagram for the SYSTEM subdirectory (see above diagram) the command would be TREE \WINDOWS\SYSTEM
Another way of doing this would be to change to the appropriate directory and then issue the command. *You do not need to give a path if you are in the same directory as the files that you want to work with.*

5. Now, making sure that you are in the root directory of C drive, issue the two above commands:

TREE \WINDOWS

TREE \WINDOWS\SYSTEM

You will probably get the message that there are no subdirectories in the SYSTEM subdirectory. On large hard disks the pathnames can get quite complicated – 4 levels of subdirectory are not uncommon, eg \SALES\MARCH\LETTERS\JM

6. **Error messages.** Change to the root directory if necessary and try out the following syntax errors;

Type **DIR WINDOW**

You get the message 'File not found' as you misspelled the name of the WINDOWS directory.

Type **DIRWINDOWS**

You get the error message 'Bad command or file name' as you omitted the space between the command and the parameter.

Type DIR / W

You get an 'Invalid switch' error message as there should be no space following the / symbol.

Activity 4   Sorting files – the 'O' switch

Introduction

Now that we have a better understanding of MS-DOS syntax we can extend our use of the DIR command and use further switches to look through directories and sort files into particular orders.

1. Type **HELP DIR** The formal command syntax for the DIR command is given as follows –

    DIR [drive:][path][filename] [/P] [/W] [/A[[:]attributes]]

    [/O[[:]sortorder]] [/S] [/B] [/L]

    Even those who understand MS-DOS syntax can find this daunting, however you'll never need to remember and use them all – the Help facility is always there to remind you. Just remember that you don't type the square brackets – they denote optional items the forward slash / denotes a switch

2. It is possible to sort the files in a directory listing into a number of useful orders, eg by creation date or by file size. This is the meaning of the [/O[[:]sortorder]] part of the syntax. /O is the switch followed by a secondary switch letter. There are 5 pairs in all

    /ON files and directories listed alphabetically (a- z)

    /O-N files and directories listed reverse alphabetically (z – a)

    /OE files and directories listed in order of extension

    /O-E files and directories listed in reverse order of extension

    /OS files and directories listed in order of size

    /O-S files and directories listed in reverse order (largest first)

    /OD files and directories listed, oldest first

    /O-D files and directories listed, latest first

    /OG alphabetically a-z with directories listed first

    /O-G alphabetically a-z with directories listed last

Examples:

    DIR /ON

    DIR /O-N

    DIR /OG

130

Notes: The minus sign (-) is used to reverse the order of the switch

You can only use one O switch at a time, eg if you typed DIR /OE/OD the first one would be ignored

The O switch can be combined with the /W and /P switches, in any order eg DIR /OE/P or DIR /P/OE

Make sure that you use the letter 'o' or 'O' not the number zero '0'.

3. Change to the WINDOWS subdirectory and issue the following commands. (you can add the /W or /P switch to stop the display scrolling)

    DIR /O-N the files and subdirectory names are listed in reverse order

    DIR /OE all files with common extensions are grouped together – see Unit 10, Activity 7 for an explanation of these. Note that directories get listed first as they have no extensions.

    DIR /OG the same as the default DIR command, but directories are displayed first – useful in locating directories.

4. Now use the /O-D switch to display the most recently created file/directories first. This is very useful if you cannot remember the filename but have an idea of the date it was created (or amended).

5. Now use the /OS switch to display the smallest files first. Notice that directories are not given a size under MS-DOS so appear first.

6. If you have access to a printer you can experiment with ending the DIR command with >PRN This will redirect the directory listing from the screen to the printer.

7. **Hint – cancelling a DIR command.** You may wish to cancel a DIR command before it is completed. Any DOS command can be cancelled by holding down the Ctrl key and typing the letter C

Activity 5   Searching for files using wild card characters

Introduction

In the previous activity we learnt how to sort files in a directory into various different orders. Often we want to be more selective and only display certain files, eg only files with a particular extension.

The * or 'star' symbol is used in many DOS commands as a 'wildcard' character to stand for any combination of characters, eg:

*.EXE means any file name ending in the extension .EXE

JIM.* means all files with the name JIM and ending in any extension

131

JIM*.* means that the first 3 characters of the file name must be JIM, the rest of the file name and the extension can be anything.

The ? symbol is used to substitute for individual characters, this is more precise and needs greater care in its use, eg:

???AUG.COM means that the first three characters of the file name can be anything, the final three letters must be AUG, and the extension must be .COM

*.JM? means that the file name can be anything, the first two characters of the extension must be JM, and the third character can be anything.

1. Make sure that you are in the WINDOWS subdirectory.

   Issue the command **DIR *.EXE**

   All the files with the .EXE (pronounced 'dot exee') extension, ie program files, are listed. Notice that the total disk space occupied by these files is given at the bottom of the listing. This can be useful if you are considering freeing up space on your disk.

2. Issue the command **DIR CAL*.***

   All the files beginning with the three characters CAL are listed, including the program (.EXE) and help (.HLP) files for the Windows Calculator and Calendar accessories. If they are not listed it may be that these accessories have been deleted from your copy of Windows.

3. **Independent activity**

   You wish to list files associated with printing, List all the files beginning in PRI
   If you are connected to a printer then use the >PRN parameter to print off the listing.

4. We want to list the files with the extension .GRP and .HLP We can use the ? symbol to indicate that the the first two letters of the extension can be any character but the third must be a 'P'.

   Type the command **DIR *.??P**

   All the files with these extensions are listed, to stop them scrolling off the screen we need to add the /W or /P switch – try this.

5. **Repeating the previous command – the F1 and F3 keys**

   Press the F3 key and the previous command is recalled. Press Enter and the previous command is executed. This avoids re-typing complex commands if you need to correct or amend them. You can use the Backspace key to erase characters from the end of the command.

   try the following:

   Issue the command **DIR *.S??**

   Now press the **F3** key and add the switch **/OS**

Re-issue the command by pressing Enter.

The **F1** key will repeat the previous command a letter at a time. This is useful if you wish to change individual characters.

Use the F1 key to amend the previous command to **DIR *.S??/W**

6. **The Doskey facility**

This feature allows you to recall all previously used commands, as well as offering better editing features.

Type the command **DOSKEY** – if it has not already been installed you get the message 'DOSKey installed'.

Continue with the next activity, we will use Doskey to recall future commands.

7. **Independent activity**

Issue the command to list all files with either the extension .DAT or .DLL

8. **Searching More than one directory – the /S Switch.**

All the previous wildcard searches were confined to one directory – the WINDOWS subdirectory. If you need to look through more than one directory for files of a particular type you can use the /S switch.

Change to the root directory using the CD\ command.

Now issue the command **DIR *.HLP/S**

All the files on disk with the extension .HLP are listed, under their directory and subdirectory names. The /S switch can locate files any where in the directory tree, and is very useful in tracking down missing or duplicated files.

As before you can use the /W or /P switches to stop the listing scrolling off screen, or >PRN to print it.

Activity 6 Searching for files by attribute – the /A switch

Every file has 4 attributes or features which can be set on or off -

r indicates read-only – the file is protected from amendment,

h indicates hidden – the file is not normally listed in a directory listing.

s indicates system file – it is part of the computer's operating system,

a indicates archive – it is used with certain MS-DOS copy commands to control whether a file is backed up.

133

Some of these are only of practical importance with key system files, which are hidden, read-only and marked with a special system designator. We'll briefly review these.

1. Display the help text for the DIR command again. You will see that the syntax includes a switch for listing files by attribute – [/A[[:]attributes]]. Like the sort switch it consists of a switch (/A) followed by another secondary switch letter. The minus sign

   (-) is used to list files not having the attribute, ie

   /AH hidden files

   /A-H non-hidden files

   /AS MS-DOS system files

   /A-S not MS-DOS system file

   /AR read only files

   /A-R updateable, amendable files

   /AA Files requiring archiving or backup

   /A-A file unchanged since last backup

   Another useful attribute identifies a directory or a file:

   /AD directories listed only

   /A-D files only

2. Make sure you are in the root directory and type the command

   DIR /AH

   Two hidden system files are displayed, IO.SYS and MSDOS.SYS.

3. Now issue the commands **DIR /AS** and **DIR /AR** – the same two files are displayed. Because of their fundamental importance in running MS-DOS these two files have their attributes set to hidden, read only and system.

4. Type the command **DIR /AD** – a list of directories only is made.

5. Type the command **DIR /AA** which shows the list of files needing backing up. A newly created or an amended file has the archive attribute set on to alert you that it needs backing up. We will be using this feature later.

6. Now use the Up Arrow key. You will find that the DOSKEY program that you ran in Activity 5 has saved your previous commands. They can be re-issued or amended as required. You will find it a useful shortcut. Remember that the DOSKEY utility has normally to be run every time you start DOS.

Activity 7 Independent directory activities

To round up the previous directory activities try the following for further practice. Sections 1 and 2 are machine-based. Sections 3 and 4 are paper-based and solutions are given in Appendix 3.

1. Change to the DOS subdirectory.
   a. How many .EXE files are they?
   b. Which .EXE file is the largest?
   c. List all files whose extensions begin with C .
   d. List in alphabetical order all files whose names begin with the three letters DOS

2. Change to the root directory.
   a. List all files, directories last.
   b. List all files, oldest first. What is the date of the oldest?

3. What do the following DIR commands do?
   a. DIR \WINDOWS*.HLP /ON/P
   b. DIR *.?C? /S
   c. In the command 3a, identify the command name, the path name, the file name and the switches.
   d. Identify three syntax errors in the command
      DIR /DOS/*.COM \W and put them right.

4. Look at Figure 3 on page 124.
   a. If you are in the root directory what command would you give to change to the the SYSTEM subdirectory of the WINDOWS subdirectory?
   b. What command changes you from the SYSTEM subdirectory to the DOS subdirectory?
   c. How would you return to the root directory?
   d. If you are in the root directory what command would you give to display the directory tree for the WINDOWS subdirectory, including its files, sending it to the printer?

Summary of commands

Notes:

Optional elements of commands are shown in square brackets [ ]
Do **not** include these square brackets when you type the command, they are only there to guide you.

Commands may be typed in uppercase or lowercase.

All commands must be followed by pressing the Enter Key

*	Represent any number of characters in a file name/extension, eg DIR *.TXT
?	Represent single character in a file name/extension, eg DIR LET??. T??
CD [drive:][directory name]	Change to named directory
CD..	Go up one directory level
CD\	Change to root directory
Ctrl-C	Cancel an MS-DOS command
TREE[/A][/F][drive:][directory name]	Display the directory tree, the /F switch displays files in subdirectories as well, the /A switch ensures that lines linking subdirectories are printed
DIR /O[sort order]	Display directory listing in a variety of orders – see Activity 4
DIR [drive:][directory name] file name/S	Searches all subdirectories of current directory for specified file name

136

Creating, moving and copying files

Introduction

In this unit you will create some files then copy and move them into directories that you have created to hold them.

Skills covered	Activity
Directory – creating	3
Directory – removing	3
Editor – using	1
Files – copying and moving	4, 5
Files – saving	1
Wild Cards (/ and *) – Using	5

Previous skills required	Covered in unit
Starting MS-DOS	Units 10 and 11)
Issuing MS-DOS commands	
Formatting a diskette	

Resources required

Two formatted diskettes

Activity 1 Creating some simple text files

Introduction

For your future MS-DOS activities you will need a set of files for you to practice such skills as moving, copying, deleting etc. These files will be 'dummy' files, meaning that what they contain doesn't matter. If you have completed the Windows part of these units then you have already created these files using Windows Notepad. However they will need to be in the root directory, not subdirectories. (Lecturers using these units as a course text can obtain these files on disk from the publishers – see preface)

We are going to use the MS-DOS Edit program – this is a text editor. Like the Windows Notepad application it can be to create simple text documents, including programs and batch files. You can cut, copy and paste text but it lacks word processing features such as page setup, fonts etc.

We are going to create the practice files on the system diskette that you prepared in Unit 10, Activity 5. Even if you already have these files you may wish to create them again in order to to learn more about the MS-DOS Editor.

1. **Troubleshooting**

    The MS-DOS Editor program is located in the DOS subdirectory, but can normally be run whichever drive and dirctory you are using. If you find that this is not the case then you will have to change to the DOS subdirectory before you run it.

2. Put the disk that you formatted in Unit 10, Activity 5 in the diskette drive.

    Check that A is the current active drive, if not type A: to change.

    The MS-DOS prompt should now read A:\>

3. Issue the command EDIT and the Editor screen appears, overlaid with a welcome message – read this. If you are not familiar with text or word processors then press Enter and read the Survival Guide; otherwise press the Esc key and carry on.

4. The Editor has Windows type features such as mouse and pull-down menus. I shall be giving instructions for mouse operations, but, as we will see, you can use the keyboard instead. (you may need to use the keyboard if your mouse is not enabled for DOS)

5. A flashing cursor indicates the insertion point for text. Now simply type a few lines of text. If your typing skills are minimal simply fill up the lines with a jumble of characters. There is no automatic word wrap feature to move you along to the next line, so press the Enter key when you get to the end of the line.

6. **Saving a new file.** At the moment the text that you have created is only saved in the computer's main memory. It has the temporary name 'Untitled' and will be lost as soon as you exit the Editor unless you save it as a named file.

    At the top of the Editor screen are a series of pull-down menus – File, Edit, Search, Options.

    Mouse method

    Use the mouse to move the screen pointer onto the **File** menu.

Click the left hand mouse button once and a series of options are displayed.

Move the pointer onto the **Save As** option and click the left hand mouse button.

Keyboard method

Press the **Alt** key on the keyboard – you can then use the left and right arrow keys to select each menu – try this.

Select the **File** menu and press **Enter;** a series of options are displayed. Each has a highlighted letter that is used to select it.

Type **A** for the Save as option.

7. The Save As dialogue box appears next. You can either use the mouse to select and execute the option you want or use the Tab and Return keys.

    a. The **File Name** box is selected at the moment. Look at the **Dirs/Drives** box, it shows the available drives and directories, we want to save this file onto A drive.

    b. Find the A drive, if it is not visible then use the down arrow key. Select the A drive using the mouse or the Enter key.

        The File Name box now shows A: as the active drive

    c. Now select the File Name box and type the file name MEMSAL1.TXT (upper or lower case). If you have made a mistake you can use the Cancel option to start again; if you need further help then take the Help option.

    d. Finally click the **OK** box. The command is executed and the file MEMSAL1.TXT is saved to diskette, the drive light comes on to show that the data is being written (saved) to disk.

        The dialogue box disappears and you are returned to the Editor screen which now displays the file name of the newly saved file MEMSAL1.TXT.

8. **Saving changes**

    Add a few more lines of text to this file. These changes will need saving permanently to disk too.

    Open the **File** menu; this time choose the **Save** option. *(not Save as)* The drive light comes on again indicates that the changes are being permanently saved to to the MEMSAL1.TXT file on disk.

9. **Saving a file under a new name**

    Add a few more lines of text to the file; open the **File** menu again, but this time choose the **Save As** option.

    The Save As dialogue box appears.

    Make sure that the Dirs/Drives: box still shows **A:** and amend the file name to MEMSAL2.TXT

    Select the **OK** button.

The drive light comes on as before to show that the new file MEMSAL2.TXT is being written (saved) to disk.

10. The Editor screen now displays the file name MEMSAL2.TXT. The original file MEMSAL1.TXT is saved and closed and the copy opened.
Now we'll use this method again to create six more files; keep adding a few more lines of text (this means that all files will vary slightly in size), then choose Save As from the File menu.

Name the files that you create as follows:
Make sure that you name the files exactly as below and that they are saved on a drive; they will be important in our future activities.

MEMSAL3.TXT

MEMSAL4.TXT

MEMACC1.TXT

MEMACC2.TXT

MEMACC3.TXT

MEMACC4.TXT

When you have created these files open the **File** menu and select the **Open** option; you will see the 8 files listed that you created using the Editor;

11. **A note on naming conventions.**

The file naming convention used reserves the first three lettters for the type of document, MEM = memo.

Letters 4 – 6 are reserved for the department, ACC = Accounts. The final number on the file name is the order of creation and ensures that each file name is unique.

The file name is separated by a full stop from the 3 letter extension TXT. The Editor automatically assigns the extension .TXT to documents created in it.

An extension is optional for some types of files including the Editor, (one is free to use no extension at all or any other extension up to three letters or numbers) Others, eg program files, require a particular extension, eg .EXE in order to run. When you are creating files make sure that you use a meaningful, memorable naming convention and stick to it.

12. **Exiting and saving a file**

Add another line of text to the current file.

Now try to exit the Editor application as follows; open the **File** menu and select **Exit.**

A dialogue box appears, reminding you that you have not saved the changes made to the file.

Click the **Cancel** button which returns you to the document. (normally you would click the Yes button which saves and exits the document)

Now exit the Editor again, this time taking selecting the **Yes** option on the Dialogue box.

A situation where you would find it useful to click the **No** button and exit a document without saving is if you have made some major unwanted change to a document e.g. a deletion. Exiting without saving would leave the document as it was the last time it was saved, before you made the alteration.

Activity 2   Independent activity

Introduction

You have already created a number of text files using the Editor – see the previous activity; ensure that the diskette storing these files is still in A drive.

1.   Create and save the following eight dummy files onto A drive using the Editor as you did in the previous activity :-

LETSAL1.JM
LETSAL2.DOC
LETSAL3.TXT
LETSAL4.TXT
LETACC1.TXT
LETACC2.TXT
LETACC3.TXT
LETACC4.TXT

Make sure that you use exactly these names When you have created all the above files quit the Editor and return to the MS-DOS prompt.

Activity 3   Making directories

Introduction

In the previous activities we have created the following 16 dummy files, using the MS-DOS Editor:-

MEMSAL1.TXT
MEMSAL2.TXT
MEMSAL3.TXT
MEMSAL4.TXT
MEMACC1.TXT

```
                              MEMACC2.TXT
                              MEMACC3.TXT
                              MEMACC4.TXT
                              LETSAL1.JM
                              LETSAL2.DOC
                              LETSAL3.TXT
                              LETSAL4.TXT
                              LETACC1.TXT
                              LETACC2.TXT
                              LETACC3.TXT
                              LETACC4.TXT
```

The file names contain 4 elements :

The first three letters indicate the type of document, MEM = memo, LET = letter.

Letters 4 – 6 indicate the department, ACC = Accounts and SAL = Sales.

The final digit, 1,2,3 etc. on the file name indicates the order of creation and ensures that each file name is unique.

The file name is separated by a full stop from an optional 2 or 3 letter extension.

We are going to organise these files into directories and subdirectories; all the files concerned with Sales Department will be placed in a directory SALES and those concerned with the Accounts Department in a directory ACCOUNTS. within each of these directories there will be a subdirectory for memos and one for letters. The directory tree will look like this:

```
    A:.
     |------SALES
     |            MEMSAL4.TXT
     |            MEMSAL2.TXT
     |            MEMSAL3.TXT
     |            LETSAL1.JM
     |            MEMSAL1.TXT
     |            LETSAL2.DOC
     |            LETSAL3.TXT
     |            LETSAL4.TXT
     |------ACCOUNTS
                  MEMACC1.TXT
                  MEMACC2.TXT
                  MEMACC3.TXT
                  MEMACC4.TXT
                  LETACC1.TXT
                  LETACC2.TXT
                  LETACC3.TXT
                  LETACC4.TXT
```

142

Notes on directory names. Directory Names follow the same conventions as file names, except that directories do not end in an extension, ie:

A directory name can consist of up to 8 characters, these can be the letters A to Z (upper or lower case) or numbers 0 to 9.

Certain other keyboard characters can be used, including the dash (-),and the underscore character (_).

The following **cannot** be used: space, comma, full stop, slash, colon, semicolon, brackets, quotation marks and the equals sign.
You may succeed in creating directories with these invalid characters, but you are liable to lose some of the characters from the name and unpredictable results may occur when you use them.

1. Make sure that the diskette containing the above files is inserted in A drive.

    Check that A is the current active drive, if not type A: to change to A drive. The

    MS-DOS prompt should now read A:\>

2. Type DIR – the Directory window should be as follows: (the creation dates and sizes of your files will obviously differ)

    Volume in drive A has no label
    Volume Serial Number is 2E1D-16FA
    Directory of A:\

COMMAND	COM	54,645	31/05/94	6:22
MEMSAL1	TXT	242	15/08/95	16:19
MEMSAL2	TXT	296	15/08/95	16:19
MEMSAL3	TXT	313	15/08/95	16:21
MEMSAL4	TXT	342	15/08/95	16:21
MEMACC1	TXT	381	15/08/95	16:22
MEMACC2	TXT	430	15/08/95	16:23
MEMACC3	TXT	491	15/08/95	16:23
MEMACC4	TXT	602	15/08/95	16:29
LETSAL1	JM	640	15/08/95	16:31
LETSAL2	DOC	696	15/08/95	16:32
LETSAL3	TXT	752	15/08/95	16:32
LETSAL4	TXT	814	15/08/95	16:33
LETACC1	TXT	877	15/08/95	16:33
LETACC2	TXT	919	15/08/95	16:33
LETACC3	TXT	1,024	15/08/95	16:34
LETACC4	TXT	1,060	15/08/95	16:34

    17 file(s)   64,524 bytes
    1,242,624 bytes free

143

As we are using a diskette that has been formatted as a system disk (see Unit 10, Activity 5) the main DOS command processor file, COMMAND.COM, is also listed.

If the files are not displayed, check that the correct diskette is in A drive.

3. **Making directories**

   The DOS command to make a directory is simply MD. To test the rules for directory names – see above – let's try typing invalid names.

   Issue the command **MD ACC DIR** As the space is an invalid character the name is rejected.

   Now issue the command **MD SALES-FILES**

   Use the **DIR** command to check the command has worked.

   A new directory called SALES-FI is created in the root directory of A drive. DOS has given the directory the first 8 characters of the name and ignored the rest.

4. **Removing directories**

   We will now remove this wrongly-named directory and

   re-create it. The RD command is used to remove a directory.

   Issue the command **RD SALES-FI**

   Now use the DIR command to check that the directory is removed.

5. Use the MD command to make two directories, SALES and ACCOUNTS

6. Use the command DIR /OE to display the listing, directories first.

   The listing should be as shown on the following page.

```
Volume in drive A has no label
Volume Serial Number is 2E1D-16FA
Directory of A:\

        SALES                 <DIR>                15/08/95    16:47
        ACCOUNTS              <DIR>                15/08/95    16:47
        COMMAND     COM            54,645         31/05/94     6:22
        LETSAL2     DOC               696         15/08/95    16:32
        LETSAL1     JM                640         15/08/95    16:31
        MEMSAL1     TXT               242         15/08/95    16:19
        MEMSAL2     TXT               296         15/08/95    16:19
        MEMSAL3     TXT               313         15/08/95    16:21
        MEMSAL4     TXT               342         15/08/95    16:21
        MEMACC1     TXT               381         15/08/95    16:22
        MEMACC2     TXT               430         15/08/95    16:23
        MEMACC3     TXT               491         15/08/95    16:23
        MEMACC4     TXT               602         15/08/95    16:29
        LETSAL3     TXT               752         15/08/95    16:32
        LETSAL4     TXT               814         15/08/95    16:33
        LETACC1     TXT               877         15/08/95    16:33
        LETACC2     TXT               919         15/08/95    16:33
        LETACC3     TXT             1,024         15/08/95    16:34
        LETACC4     TXT             1,060         15/08/95    16:34

    19 file(s)   64,524 bytes
    1,240,064 bytes free
```

Activity 4   Moving and copying individual files

Introduction

Now we will copy and move files from A:\ the root directory into the two new subdirectories – SALES and ACCOUNTS that we have just created. Moving a file does just that – removes it to a new location, copying a file keeps the original where it is *and* places a copy in the new location. We will practice both operations using the COPY and MOVE commands.

Note: DOS 5 Users. The MOVE command is only available from DOS 6.0 onwards. DOS 5 users should therefore omit the MOVE activities, or substitute the COPY command instead. A move command is available in Windows – see Unit 6.

1. **Copying files.** Type HELP COPY to see the syntax of the COPY command.
    The command syntax looks fairly complex, but in most cases copying is straightforward. Often one wants to copy (or move) a file

to a different directory but keep the name of the file the same. MS-DOS permits duplicate file names as long as the files are not in the same directory.

Exit Help.

2. Make sure that the diskette containing the practice files is in the diskette drive, that the DOS prompt shows A as the active drive and you are in the root directory (to change drives type the letter followed by a colon, eg A:)
You will find it easier to recall and re-issue commands if you use the DOSKEY facility in this session – see Unit 11.

3. To copy the file MEMSAL4.TXT from the root to the SALES subdirectory issue the command

COPY A:\MEMSAL4.TXT A:\SALES\MEMSAL4.TXT

DOS will confirm '1 file(s) copied'.

Now issue the command DIR \SALES – the SALES directory listing now shows a copy of the MEMSAL4.TXT file.

4. **Troubleshooting**

If the command does not work check that the file and directory names and the \ and : symbols are correct. The only two spaces in the command should be after the COPY command and separating the source file path A:\MEMSAL4.TXT from the destination file path A:\SALES\MEMSAL4.TXT

5. **Simplifying the path**

The command

'COPY A:\MEMSAL4.TXT A:\SALES\MEMSAL4.TXT'

means 'copy the file

MEMSAL4.TXT from the root directory on A drive to the SALES subdirectory on A drive, naming it MEMSAL4.TXT'.

Though correct, it contained unnecessary elements; the following can be omitted from the full command syntax of the COPY and MOVE commands (and many other commands):

a. the current active drive and directory names.

b. the destination file name if you are not renaming it

c. the directory name if copying takes place within the same directory.

As conditions a and b apply, the command can simply be,

COPY MEMSAL4.TXT \SALES

Issue this command. DOS will prompt you:

Overwrite A:\SALES\MEMSAL4.TXT (Yes/No/All)?

This is to confirm that when you copy the same file twice you want the original copy to be overwritten.

Type Y (plus Enter) and DOS confirms '1 file copied'.

146

6. **Independent activity**

   Use the COPY command to copy the files MEMSAL2.TXT and MEMSAL3.TXT to the SALES subdirectory.

   Use the command DIR \SALES to check that the files were copied to the correct subdirectory.

7. **Moving files** (MS-DOS 6 only) Issue the command

   MOVE LETSAL1.JM \SALES

   DOS confirms the file name, the move operation and the destination subdirectory.

   Using the DIR command will check that the file has been removed from the root directory and placed in the SALES subdirectory.

   You should now have 4 files in the SALES subdirectory.

Activity 5   Moving and copying groups of files

Introduction

Often one wants to move a group of related files to a new location. This is simple using the wild card characters * and ? we learnt using the DIR command – see Unit 11, Activity 5.

To recap briefly:

The * or 'star' can stand for any number of characters;

*.WRI means any file name ending in the extension .WRI

LET*.* means a file name starting with the the three characters LET and ending in anything.

. signifies all file names (any name, any extension)

The ? symbol substitutes for individual characters; suppose that I want to copy all files containing the three characters ACC in position 4 – 6 of their file names, e.g. MEMACC1.TXT or LETACC2.WRI
The file name ???ACC?.* means 'starting with any three characters, then the characters ACC, any other character at the end, and followed by any extension (*)'

1. **Copying groups of files**

   Make sure that the diskette containing the practice files is in the diskette drive and that the DOS prompt shows A as the active drive. Make sure that you are in the root directory.

   Issue the command

   COPY ???ACC?.* \ACCOUNTS

   making sure to type each character exactly as shown.

   DOS will confirm '8 files copied'.

147

Now issue the command DIR \ACCOUNTS – the ACCOUNTS subdirectory should contain eight files:

MEMACC1.TXT

MEMACC2.TXT

MEMACC3.TXT

MEMACC4.TXT

LETACC1.TXT

LETACC2.TXT

LETACC3.TXT

LETACC4.TXT

2. **Independent activity**

We now want to copy all the files with the three characters SAL at character positions 4-6 of the file name to the SALES directory. Try and do this yourself, basing the command on the syntax of the COPY command in section 1 above.

Note: Some have already been copied – see Activity 4 above – so you will be asked to confirm that you want these copies overwritten. Answer a for all and 7 files will be copied.

3. To confirm that your copying is successful issue the TREE/F command. The diagram should be as follows, confirming that the practice files remain in the root directory (with the exception of one that was moved), and copies made to the appropriate SALES and ACCOUNTS subdirectories.

```
Directory PATH listing
Volume Serial Number is 2E1D-16FA
A:.
    COMMAND.COM
    MEMSAL1.TXT
    MEMSAL2.TXT
    MEMSAL3.TXT
    MEMSAL4.TXT
    LETSAL2.DOC
    LETSAL3.TXT
    LETSAL4.TXT
    MEMACC1.TXT
    MEMACC2.TXT
    MEMACC3.TXT
    MEMACC4.TXT
    LETACC1.TXT
    LETACC2.TXT
    LETACC3.TXT
    LETACC4.TXT

---SALES
            MEMSAL4.TXT
            MEMSAL2.TXT
            MEMSAL3.TXT
            LETSAL1.JM
            MEMSAL1.TXT
            LETSAL2.DOC
            LETSAL3.TXT
            LETSAL4.TXT

---ACCOUNTS
            MEMACC1.TXT
            MEMACC2.TXT
            MEMACC3.TXT
            MEMACC4.TXT
            LETACC1.TXT
            LETACC2.TXT
            LETACC3.TXT
            LETACC4.TXT
```

4. **Moving groups of files** (DOS 6 only)

    The MOVE command works in exactly the same way.

    Issue the command

    MOVE ???ACC?.* \ACCOUNTS

DOS will confirm that 8 files are moved from the root directory to the ACCOUNTS subdirectory.
Use the TREE/F command to check this.

Paper exercises *(answers in appendix 4)*

1. Can you create a directory called MY FILES?

2. You are in the root directory of A: drive and have 2 subdirectories called JIM and JOHN.

    Give the commands to copy:

    a. All files with the extension .TXT from JIM to JOHN

    b. All files with beginning in OLD from the root directory to JIM

3. Remove the unnecessary elements from the following command:

    COPY A:\JOHN\BUDGET.1 A:\JIM\BUDGET.1

Summary of commands

Notes:

Optional elements of commands are shown in square brackets [ ]
Do **not** include these square brackets when you type the command, they are only there to guide you.

Commands may be typed in uppercase or lowercase.

All commands must be followed by 'Enter'.

COPY source destination	The source file name(s) must be included, other details of drive, path destination name may sometimes be omitted – see Activity 3
EDIT [drive:][path][file name]	Edit text file using MS-DOS editor
MD [drive:][path][directory name]	Create directory
MOVE source destination	See COPY command
RD [drive:][path][directory name]	Remove directory

unit 13

Disk copying, renaming files and file attributes

Introduction

In this unit you will be learning some more important file management skills – copying files between disk drives, copying files between subdirectories, copying disks, renaming files and setting file attributes.

Skills covered	Activity
Diskettes – copying	3
Files – changing attributes	5
Files – copying between disk drives	1
Files – copying between subdirectories	2
Files – copying and renaming	1.7
Files – protecting	5
Files – renaming	4

Previous skills required	Covered in units
Starting MS-DOS	(see Units 10 and 11)
Issuing MS-DOS commands	
Formatting a diskette	

Resources required

The diskette containing the practice files plus another formatted diskette

151

Activity 1 Copying files between disk drives

Introduction

Most users need to copy files between disks in the following situations;

    a. Taking backup copies of important program or data files from the hard disk to diskette in case the originals are lost or destroyed.

    b. Similarly copying files from one diskette to another.

    c. Transferring files from a diskette to hard disk. Because of the ever-present threat of viruses most colleges do not allow this, and/or prevent it by technical means.

I shall therefore be concentrating on a and b; if you are using your PC at home you may wish to try c, the principle is the same.

Similarly I shall be concentrating on the COPY command and its variants not the MOVE command which, if used incorrectly, could remove vital files from your hard disk.

1. Write-protecting diskettes

You have created some files on your practice disk that need backing up; you will need a second formatted diskette which to use for this. Create this now if necessary, using Unit 10, Activity 5 as a guide.

First we need to make sure that we can tell the two disks apart. Take the practice disk and open the write-protect notch. A small square hole appears, the disk is now 'read-only', meaning that it can be read and copied but not overwritten – until you close the notch.

Now write on the disk practice **disk a (source)**

Take the second practice disk and write on it **practice disk b (target)** but keep the write-protect notch closed.

2. Copying individual files from one diskette to another

Assuming that the diskette containing the practice files is in the diskette drive and that the DOS prompt shows A as the active drive, let's try a fairly simple copy operation first – copying a file from the root directory to the second disk.

Issue the command

    COPY A:\MEMSAL1.TXT B:

Although there is no B drive DOS treats A drive as two separate drives, A and B.

(If you have two diskette drives then the operation is simpler as you can place your second diskette in drive B. The instructions that follow assume that you only have one diskette drive)

3. DOS prompts you to:

    Insert diskette for drive B: and strike any key when ready.

    Insert practice disk b and press a key.

    You will be prompted to insert the SOURCE a: disk next. Do so and press a key.

4. You may have to repeat these steps a few more times – this depends on the number and size of files being copied. When copying is complete the A:\> prompt appears again.

5. Use the DIR command to check that the file has been copied to the practice disk b.

6. **Copying multiple files from one diskette to another**

    The principle is the same as before, except that you use wild card operators to identify the files that you wish to copy.

    Insert practice disk a in the disk drive and issue the command;

    COPY A:\???SAL?.* B:

    The DOS prompts are the same as before, but because you are copying more files you will have to swap the disks over more times than before.

    When you have finished these activities remember to close the write-protect notch on practice disk a, otherwise you will be unable to add, delete, or modify its contents.

7. **Copying and renaming a file**

    Make sure that practice disk a is in the diskette drive. Change to C drive and check that the two files AUTOEXEC.BAT and CONFIG.SYS are in the root directory. If not choose another small file in the root directory to copy.

    We are going to make a backup copy of the AUTOEXEC.BAT file FROM C drive onto diskette, renaming it AUTOEXEC.BAK. Issue the command;

    COPY C:\AUTOEXEC.BAT A:\AUTOEXEC.BAK

    DOS should confirm '1 file copied'.

8. Now make another copy of AUTOEXEC.BAK, renaming it AUTOEXEC.NEW

9. Next copy the file CONFIG.SYS from C to A drive, renaming it CONFIG.BAK.

153

Activity 2 Copying between subdirectories

Introduction

If we assume that the ACCOUNTS subdirectory holds files relevant to an Accounts Department and the SALES subdirectory those relevant to a Sales Department, there will be occasions when we need to copy (or move) files from one to another. As we will see it is vital to get the path right when we are doing this, otherwise the file will not be copied, or be copied to the wrong directory.

1. Make sure that practice disk a is in the diskette drive, that A is the active drive and that you are in the root directory. We are going to copy the file MEMACC1.TXT from the ACCOUNTS to the SALES subdirectory.

   Let's see what can go wrong first – you will find it useful to set Doskey on for this activity in order to re-issue commands.

2. Issue the command

   COPY MEMACC1.TXT \SALES

   The error message 'file not found' is displayed. The command, the file name and extension are correct but you haven't given the path to the file that you want to copy, ie told DOS where the file is. You are in the root directory but the file is in the ACCOUNTS subdirectory – DOS doesn't know this! Unless you are already in the directory or subdirectory which holds the file, you must give the directory name as part of the command.

3. Modify the command to

   COPY ACCOUNTS\MEMACC1.TXT \SALES

   This time you should get the message '1 file copied'.

4. Issue the command **CD \SALES** to change to the SALES subdirectory. Use the DIR command to check that the file is successfully copied.

5. Now for an even more baffling error! Remain in the SALES subdirectory and issue the command

   COPY LETSAL1.JM ACCOUNTS

   DOS confirms '1 file copied'. Now change to the ACCOUNTS subdirectory and use DIR to check that it has been copied – it's not there!

   Change back to the SALES subdirectory and check there – you will see a file listed named ACCOUNTS. You may now see what has gone wrong, your COPY command did not give the full path to the destination directory ACCOUNTS. The ACCOUNTS subdirectory is in the root directory and a \ symbol in front of the directory name should have indicated this.

DOS failed to find the ACCOUNTS subdirectory so instead 'assumed' that you wanted to copy the file as a new file ACCOUNTS.

Delete the file called ACCOUNTS using the command

DEL ACCOUNTS

Check that it has been deleted.

6. Modify the command to

COPY LETSAL1.JM \ACCOUNTS

and check that the file has been copied successfully this time.

7. Change to the root directory.

Activity 3 *Copying entire disks – the XCOPY command*

Introduction

Next we will copy the two subdirectories on practice disk a – SALES and ACCOUNTS – and the files that they contain to practice disk b. This would be a laborious process using the COPY command. We will use the DOS extended copy command instead – XCOPY.

1. Type

HELP XCOPY

You will see that the switches /S and /E, when used together, will copy subdirectories and their contents. XCOPY used without switches will only copy the contents of the root directory.

Exit Help.

2. Make sure that the diskette practice disk a is in the diskette drive and that the DOS prompt shows A: as the active drive.

Make sure that you are in the root directory.

Issue the command

XCOPY A: B: /S/E

Note that there are two spaces in the command – one after each colon.

As in the previous activity you are prompted to change the diskettes over.

As some of the files have already been copied you will be prompted whether you wish to overwrite the originals. Type A (plus Enter) to overwrite them all.

When the copying is complete, insert the target disk, practice disk b and use the TREE/F command to check that the subdirectories and their contents have been copied.

Note: **XCOPY versus DISKCOPY.** the command DISKCOPY will also make an identical copy of one disk to another. Unlike XCOPY, DISKCOPY will erase any files already on the target disk. This is because it copies byte by byte, rather than file by file. It is useful for copying system disks as it copies hidden system files, which XCOPY does not. The Windows 3.11 version of the copy command is equivalent to DISKCOPY

Activity 4 Renaming files

Introduction

We have seen that you can rename files when you are copying them. Sometimes we may need to rename the original without creating a copy.

The syntax of the rename command is

REN [DRIVE:][PATH:] OLDNAME NEWNAME

As before, the drive and path may be omitted if they are the current ones. You cannot specify a new drive or directory for the renamed file.

1. Make sure that practice disk b is in the diskette drive, that A is the active drive and that you are in the root directory.

   We will rename the AUTOEXEC.BAK file AUTOEXEC.OLD – often we may wish to distinguish between different copies of system files.

2. Issue the command

   REN AUTOEXEC.BAK AUTOEXEC.OLD

   Use the **DIR AUTO*.*** command to check the renaming has occurred. You should now have two versions – AUTOEXEC.NEW and the renamed AUTOEXEC.OLD

3. Let's see what happens if you try to rename a file and use a name of a file that already exists in the same directory.

   Issue the command

   REN AUTOEXEC.OLD AUTOEXEC.NEW

   Because AUTOEXEC.NEW already exists in the root directory DOS displays the error message 'Duplicate file name or file not found'.

4. It is also possible to rename a group of files, using the wildcard operators ? and *. We have the following practice files in the root directory:

   MEMSAL1.TXT

   MEMSAL2.TXT

   MEMSAL3.TXT

   MEMSAL4.TXT

156

LETSAL2.DOC

LETSAL3.TXT

LETSAL4.TXT

Duplicate copies of these exist in the SALES subdirectory – see Unit 12 – but we might well want to keep them temporarily, renaming them to avoid confusion.

Issue the command **REN *.TXT *.BAK**

Using the DIR command you will see that the files with extension .TXT have been given the BAK extension.

5. Rename file LETSAL2.DOC individually with the .BAK extension.

Activity 5   File attributes – protecting and hiding files

Introduction

A file can have a number of attributes or special features attached to it. We used the DIR command to investigate some of these – see Unit 11, Activity 6. In this activity we will practice setting them on and off, in particular the read-only and hidden attributes.

You can use these attributes to protect vital files. Making a file read-only protects it from alteration or deletion. If you want to prevent a file from being read then the hidden file attribute means that it is not listed in the disk directory; this helps to protect it from casual snoopers.

The syntax of the ATTRIB command is:

ATTRIB [ATTRIBUTES] [DRIVE:][PATH][FILENAME] [/S]

The attribute switch is set on with a + sign and removed with a -sign.

The /S switch will process not only files in the current directory but also in the subdirectories that it contains.

If the path is omitted then only files in the current drive/directory are processed.

ATTRIB used with no parameters displays the file attributes without changing them.

The attribute switches are:

+R   set on read-only attribute

-R   set off read-only attribute

+H   makes file a hidden file

-H   removes hidden file attribute

+S   makes file a system file

-S   removes system file attribute

+A   sets the archive attribute

-A   removes archive file attribute

We shall be practising with the first two switches; the archive switch is dealt with in the next activity. The system switch protects system files by hiding them from the directory listing – see Unit 11 Activity 6. These files typically have the extension .SYS or .INI and control the operations of the computer. You should not interfere with them.

1. In this activity we will reset the attributes of the files in the SALES subdirectory.

   Make sure that practice disk a is in the diskette drive, that A is the active drive and that you are in the root directory.

   Use the CD command to change to the SALES subdirectory.

   Issue the command **ATTRIB** The listing will resemble the following:

A	A:\SALES\MEMSAL4.TXT
A	A:\SALES\MEMSAL2.TXT
A	A:\SALES\MEMSAL3.TXT
A	A:\SALES\LETSAL1.JM
A	A:\SALES\MEMSAL1.TXT
A	A:\SALES\LETSAL2.DOC
A	A:\SALES\LETSAL3.TXT
A	A:\SALES\LETSAL4.TXT
A	A:\SALES\MEMACC1.TXT

   ATTRIB used without parameters displays the attributes of the files in the current drive/directory. All the files at the moment have their archive attribute (a) set on. Don't worry about this for the moment, we'll be using this in the next activity for backing up files.

2. First we will protect the file MEMSAL1.TXT from deletion or amendment.

   Issue the command

   ATTRIB MEMSAL1.TXT +R

   (leave a space before the + sign)

   Now issue the command ATTRIB to check that the attribute has been set.

3. Next we will try to edit the file using the MS-DOS Editor; issue the command

   EDIT MEMSAL1.TXT

   and the edit screen appears.

   Make a minor alteration, then open the **File** menu at the top of the edit screen and select **Save.** An error message appears, 'Path/File access error'. The file cannot be amended because the file's read-only attribute has been set on.

   Select the **OK** response and open the File menu again. This time exit without saving.

4. Issue the command

   DEL MEMSAL1.TXT

   DOS displays the message 'Access Denied', the read-only attribute protects the file from deletion.

5. To remove the read-only attribute issue the command

   ATTRIB MEMSAL1.TXT -R

   Now issue the command **ATTRIB** to check that the attribute has been removed.

6. **Hiding a file**

   Issue the command

   ATTRIB *.TXT +H

   Issue the DIR command and these files are no longer listed.

   Their hidden status can be revealed by typing **DIR /AH** which lists hidden files – try this.

   Note: Hidden files can still be edited and deleted – to prevent this you would need to make them read-only as well.

7. To remove the hidden attribute type

   ATTRIB *.TXT -H

   Type **DIR** and they are back in the listing.

8. **Independent activity**

   Change to the root directory of your practice disk and use the /S switch to set all the files to system files.

   Use the DIR /AR command to check that the file attributes have been set to system file.

   Finally remove the system file attribute.

Summary of commands

Notes:

Optional elements of commands are shown in square brackets [ ]
Do not include these square brackets when you type the command, they are only there to guide you.

Commands may be typed in uppercase or lowercase.

All commands must be followed by pressing the Enter Key.

ATTRIB   Checks file attributes or sets them on or off (see activity 5)

REN [drive:][path] old name new name

                                Renames file(s)

159

XCOPY source [destination] [/s] [/e]

Copies both files and the directory structure Source must include either a drive or a path. /s copies subdirectories, unless empty /e following /s copies empty subdirectories

Further file management activities

Introduction

In this unit you will be learning further file management skills including backing up, deleting and undeleting files and removing directories.

Skills Covered	Activity
Directories – deleting	3
Files – backing up	1
Files – deleting	2
Files – displaying Contents	4
Files – printing Contents	4
Files – restoring	1
Files – undeleting	2

Previous skills required

Starting MS-DOS   (see Units 10 and 11)
Issuing MS-DOS commands

Resources required

The diskette containing the practice files plus another formatted diskette.

Activity 1   Backing up and restoring files

Introduction

We have learnt to copy:

a.   all the files in a particular directory

b.   all files on a particular disk

161

c.   all files with a particular name or extension.

However, if we are taking backup copies of large numbers of files we may only want to copy those files:

d.   that have changed since the last time they were backed up, or,

e.   that have been amended since a certain date.

There are two DOS commands that will let us do this – XCOPY and BACKUP.

BACKUP vs XCOPY

If you are copying large numbers of files from hard disk you will need to use several diskettes. In such situations you would want the operating system to detect when a diskette is full and prompt you to insert the next one. This is an advantage of the BACKUP command over the XCOPY command – you can create a well-ordered set of backup diskettes.

However the BACKUP and its companion command RESTORE have certain practical limitations. Firstly they some involve fairly complex procedures (although the DOS 6 version simplifies them to some extent) Secondly the increasing size of files on hard disk means that using diskettes as your backup medium becomes increasingly impractical – it would take too long and use too many diskettes. Increasingly business, educational institutions and even home users are using tape for mass off-line storage.

Although is feasible to use BACKUP to copy files from hard disk to diskette, for the purposes of these units we will stick to XCOPY and demonstrate it using your two practice disks.

If we are taking backups at regular intervals there is no point in copying files that have not changed since the last backup. You can use the file archive attribute to determine this – when a file is created or changed its archive attribute A is set on. Another way is to include the file creation/modification date in the XCOPY command.

The XCOPY has the following switches:

/M   copy files with the archive attribute set on and then turn the archive attribute off

/A   copy files with the archive attribute set on and keep the archive attribute set on

/D: date copy files created or modified on or after this date.

Using XCOPY without switches means that the copying will take place unconditionally – see Unit 13.

1.   Make sure that practice disk a is in the diskette drive, that A is the active drive and that you are in the root directory. We will be using practice disk b as well in this activity.

2.   Type the command **ATTRIB -A**

All the files in the root directory of practice disk a now have the archive attribute set off. (if your diskette is a system disk then you

162

will get a message that certain hidden system files are not being reset – this is normal)

3. We still have the following practice files in the root directory, these now have their archive attribute set off. We will modify one of them:

   MEMSAL1.TXT

   MEMSAL2.TXT

   MEMSAL3.TXT

   MEMSAL4.TXT

   LETSAL2.DOC

   LETSAL3.TXT

   LETSAL4.TXT

   Issue the command **EDIT MEMSAL1.TXT** (or any other suitable text file on your diskette)

   When the Edit screen appears make some small alteration to the file, save it and exit the Editor.

4. Issue the command **ATTRIB**

   As the file MEMSAL1.TXT has been modified it has its archive attribute set on.

5. Now issue the command **XCOPY A: B: /M**

   DOS prompts you to:

   Insert diskette for drive B: and strike any key when ready

   Insert practice disk b and press a key.

   You will be prompted to insert the diskette for drive A next. Do so and press a key.

6. You may have to repeat these steps a few more times.

   If you already have a copy of a file on diskette b you will be prompted whether you wish to overwrite the original. Type Y (plus Enter) to overwrite it.

   When copying is complete the A:\> prompt appears again.

   Make sure that practice disk a is in the drive and issue the command **ATTRIB**

   This will confirm that the archive attribute a has been set off for the file MEMSAL1.TXT now that it has been copied. Unless you modify the file before your next backup it will remain off and the file will not be copied by an XCOPY command that uses the /M switch.

7. Use the DIR command to check that the file MEMSAL1.TXT has been copied to the practice disk b.

Activity 2 Deleting and undeleting files

Introduction

In this activity we will practice removing individual and groups of files from practice disk b. We will also find out how to restore deleted files using the UNDELETE command.

When you delete a file the file itself is not immediately deleted, only the reference to it in the disk directory. This is done by erasing the first character of the filename. Eventually the space used by the file will be allocated to other files. So provided you act on an accidental deletion quickly before the space is re-used, you should be able to recover the file(s).

1. Make sure that practice disk b is in the diskette drive, that A is the active drive and that you are in the root directory.

    We have the following practice files in the root directory:

    MEMSAL1.TXT

    MEMSAL2.TXT

    MEMSAL3.TXT

    MEMSAL4.TXT

    LETSAL2.DOC

    LETSAL3.TXT

    LETSAL4.TXT

    Use the DIR command to check this. Duplicate copies of these also exist in the SALES subdirectory – see Unit 13 Activity 2 – so we can delete the ones in the root directory.

2. **Deleting one file**

    Issue the command **DEL MEMSAL1.TXT**

    Now use the DIR command to check that the file is deleted

3. **Deleting a group of files**

    Even with an undelete facility it is best to double check first before deleting. One way is to use the /P switch which prompts you for confirmation before any file is deleted.

    We will delete all the files in the root directory with the extension .TXT

    Issue the command **DEL *.TXT /P**

    DOS will prompt you for a Y or N response before deleting each file.

    Ensure that each file has the extension .TXT and, if so, answer Y.

    Finally use the DIR command to check that all files with the .TXT extension are deleted.

4. Removing all the files in a directory

This is a fairly drastic step and you should check, as before, that you are not accidentally deleting the wrong files. A quicker way than the /P switch, is first to list the files.

Type **DIR *.***

This displays all the remaining files in the root directory – check that the list only contains the practice files.

Now type **DEL** and press the F3 key. This inserts the rest of the command correctly, your command should now read DEL *.*

Press Enter to execute this command.

DOS asks 'Are you sure, (Y/N)? when you use the *.* parameter. This is your last chance to back out!
We have already checked using the DIR command so answer Y

Use the DIR command to check that all the files have been deleted from the root directory. All that should be left are the two subdirectories SALES and ACCOUNTS. The listing will be as follows:

Volume in drive A has no label
Directory of A:\

ACCOUNTS	<DIR>	22/08/95	4:21
SALES	<DIR>	22/08/95	4:13

2 file(s)   0 bytes
1,158,144 bytes free

5. Undeleting files

UNDELETE can be used to recover specific files or a group of files. This facility should not be used as a substitute for taking regular backups! UNDELETE cannot for example restore a deleted file if it was in a deleted subdirectory.

6. First issue the command **UNDELETE /LIST**

All the files that we have just deleted from practice disk b should be listed. The listing will be as follows:

```
Directory: A:\
    File Specifications: *.*
    Delete Sentry control file not found.
    Deletion-tracking file not found.
    MS-DOS directory contains 41 deleted files.
    Of those, 39 files may be recovered.

Using the MS-DOS directory method.
    ?EMSAL1      TXT      241  23/08/95      17:27 ...A
    ?ETSAL2      DOC      696  15/08/95      16:32 ...A
    ?ETSAL3      TXT      752  15/08/95      16:32 ...A
    ?ETSAL4      TXT      814  15/08/95      16:33 ...A
    ?UTOEXEC     BAK      282  14/12/94      22:03 ...A
    ?UTOEXEC     NEW      282  14/12/94      22:03 ...A
    ?ONFIG       BAK      268  14/12/94      22:03 ...A
    ?ETSAL2      TXT      696  15/08/95      16:32 ...A
    ?EMSAL2      TXT      296  15/08/95      16:19 ...A
    ?EMSAL3      TXT      313  15/08/95      16:21 ...A
    ?EMSAL4      TXT      342  15/08/95      16:21 ...A
    ?EMACC1      TXT      381  15/08/95      16:22 ...A
    ?EMACC2      TXT      228  19/05/95       9:35 ...A
    ?EMACC3      TXT      258  19/05/95       9:36 ...A
    ?EMACC4      TXT      280  19/05/95       9:36 ...A
```

"**" indicates the first cluster of the file is unavailable and cannot be recovered with the UNDELETE command.

Notice that the first character of the filename is replaced by a ? If you have previously used the disk for other activities then you may well see other deleted files listed.

Issue the command

UNDELETE MEMSAL1.TXT

DOS responds with the message:

```
Directory: A:\
    File Specifications: MEMSAL1
    Deletion-tracking file not found.
    MS-DOS directory contains 1 deleted files.
    Of those, 1 files may be recovered.
    Using the MS-DOS directory.
        ?EMSAL1   24   3/01/80    13:47 ...A Undelete (Y/N)?
    Please type the first character for ?EMSAL1
```

7. Type **Y.**

You need to provide the first character of the file name.

Type **M** and you will get the message

'File successfully undeleted.'

Sometimes a file cannot be undeleted, if so proceed with the next section,

8. If there are a list of files to be undeleted, or you can't remember the file names, then UNDELETE is used without any parameters.

   Type the command UNDELETE and you are offered a list of files to be undeleted. Provide the first character as before and eventually all the deleted files will be undeleted.

   Use DIR to compare the list of recovered files with the list in section 1.

9. **Note – higher levels of file recovery**

   The UNDELETE command in MS-DOS 5 also offers Tracker, a deletion-tracking file, this file note the names of up to 200 deleted files, saving you the effort of remembering the first character of the filename. The MIRROR command is used to load Tracker. Tracker cannot recover files where the space occupied by the deleted files has already been re-used.

   MS-DOS 6 offers Sentry which keeps deleted files in a special hidden subdirectory SENTRY which is virtually impossible to delete.

   These two higher levels are especially appropriate to a hard disk if accidental deletion is likely and the consequences are serious.

Activity 3   Removing a directory containing files

Introduction

The standard RD command will not remove a directory that contains files or other subdirectories. Nor will DOS allow you to remove a directory that you are currently in. You must delete or move all the files and subdirectories from the directory before removing it. However MS-DOS 6 offers the more powerful DELTREE command that will remove a directory and its contents in one operation. This is a much quicker way of erasing unwanted directories but must be used with great care. If you are using a college machine you may find that this command has been removed from your copy of MS-DOS.

1. First we will create some practice directories and copy some files to them.
   Make sure that practice disk a is in the diskette drive, that A is the active drive and that you are in the root directory.

2. Issue the command

   MD \PRACTICE

   The subdirectory PRACTICE is created in the root directory.

   Issue the command

MD \PRACTICE\MEMOS

Issue the command

MD \PRACTICE\LETTERS

You have now created two subdirectories, MEMOS and LETTERS in the PRACTICE subdirectory.

Issue the command

TREE \PRACTICE

The tree diagram will be as follows:

```
Directory PATH listing
Volume Serial Number is 2E1D-16FA

A:\PRACTICE
    MEMOS
    LETTERS
```

3. Now to copy some files from the root directory into the MEMOS and LETTERS subdirectories. Issue the command

   COPY MEM*.* PRACTICE \MEMOS

   All the files whose names begin in MEM are copied to the MEMOS subdirectory.

   Use the **TREE \PRACTICE/F** command to check that the files are copied to the correct directory.

4. **Independent activity**

   Copy all files whose names begin in LET to the LETTERS subdirectory. The tree diagram will be as follows:

```
Directory PATH listing
Volume Serial Number is 2E1D-16FA

A:\PRACTICE
|
|----------MEMOS
|              MEMSAL1.TXT
|              MEMSAL2.TXT
|              MEMSAL3.TXT
|              MEMSAL4.TXT
|
|----------LETTERS
               LETSAL2.TXT
               LETSAL3.TXT
               LETSAL4.TXT
```

   If you have copied the files to the wrong subdirectory use the MOVE command to move them – see Unit 12, Activity 5.

5. Check that A is still the active drive and that you are in the root directory. Now let's see what happens if we try to remove these directories.

   Issue the command

   RD \PRACTICE

   DOS returns the blanket error message:

   Invalid path, not directory, or directory not empty.

   The problem is that we have tried to remove the PRACTICE directory which is not empty – it contains the MEMOS and LETTERS directories.

6. Issue the command

   RD \PRACTICE\MEMOS

   Again DOS prevents it as the MEMOS subdirectory contains a number of files.

7. Change to the MEMOS subdirectory using the

   CD \PRACTICE\MEMOS

   command.

   Now delete all the files using **DEL *.***

   Now issue the command

   RD MEMOS

   (there is no need to give the full path as memos is the current directory – the one you are in)

   Again you cannot remove the MEMOS directory as it is the current one.

   Issue the command **CD..** to go up one directory level, the DOS prompt should confirm A:\PRACTICE>

   Now repeat the command RD MEMOS This time you are successful as the two conditions are met:

   a. The directory is empty of files and subdirectories

   b. It is not the current directory.

   Change back to the root directory and use the TREE command to check that the MEMOS directory and its contents are removed.

8. The **DELTREE command**

   The PRACTICE subdirectory still contains the LETTERS subdirectory. Issue the command **DELTREE \PRACTICE**

   The PRACTICE directory and its contents are removed – check this.

   Great care should be used with this command.

Activity 4   Displaying and printing text files

Introduction

All the practice files that you have been using are ASCII text files; they contain ordinary keyboard characters plus a few other ones that are normally invisible on screen, eg carriage return and end of text markers. All PC's use the ASCII standard code (American Standard Code for Information Interchange) to represent these characters. The TYPE command will display ASCII text files on screen and the PRINT command will print them. ASCII files are normally prepared using a simple text processor such as the Windows Notepad or the MS-DOS Editor. As soon as you start creating more complex files, eg word processed documents or spreadsheets, other special codes are needed to achieve the formatting and layout, e.g. a graph display or different type styles. The TYPE and PRINT commands will not work properly on these files – you need to use the special display and printing facilities provided within the application program. Furthermore the Windows Notepad and the MS-DOS Editor provide a pull down menu containing a Print option, so there is no need to issue the PRINT command separately.

There are other types of files that TYPE and PRINT will not work with at all, especially program files with the extensions .COM and .EXE These files have been compiled, ie converted into machine code characters which the TYPE and PRINT commands cannot show correctly. However TYPE and PRINT are useful if you want to view or print a simple text file; you don't need to call up a text processor or word processor.

1.   Make sure that practice disk b is in the diskette drive, that A is the active drive and that you are in the root directory.

Type **DIR** to check what text files you have.

2.   Issue the command **TYPE** followed by the name of a suitable file-name. The contents of the file are displayed on screen.
If the file is is too long to be viewed on the screen we can stop it scrolling using the |MORE parameter – see section 5 below.

3.   Type C: to change to C drive. If necessary change to the root directory on C drive.

Now issue the command **DIR *.TXT /S/P** (you will recall – see Unit 11, Activity 5 – that the /S switch searches the current directory and all its subdirectories)

4.   All files with the extension *.TXT are listed, note down the name of one and the directory where it resides, eg a good example is any file named README.TXT, these are information files provided by the software supplier,

5.   If, say, you have a README.TXT file in the DOS subdirectory then use the TYPE command with the |MORE parameter to display it, eg:

TYPE \DOS\README.TXT|MORE

The text file will be displayed, a screenful at a time.

When you have read enough hold down the **Ctrl** key and then press **C** (Ctrl + C will always cancel a DOS command)

6. If you are connected to a printer you can try printing out this text file. Issue the command, eg, PRINT \DOS\README.TXT

   You will probably be prompted 'Name of list device [PRN]' – this is to give you the chance to change the settings, eg if you have a choice of printers. Simply press the Enter key and printing will begin.

   Notice that the MS-DOS prompt appears, the PRINT command allows multi-tasking, ie other commands can be given while printing continues in the background.

7. **Independent activity**

   The PRINT command allows a queue of files to be printed, eg PRINT FILE1.TXT FILE2.TXT

   Try this with two or more of the small text files on your practice disk.

Activity 5   Independent activity

Your practice files are now stored in two directories – **SALES** and **ACCOUNTS.**

Create two further subdirectories in each directory called **MEMOS** and **LETTERS.**

Move all files with the word **LET** in their file names to subdirectory **LETTERS**

Move all files with the word **MEM** in their file names to the subdirectory **MEMOS.**

The final structure will be as follows.

```
SALES
 |
 |---MEMOS
 |         MEMSAL1.TXT
 |         MEMSAL2.TXT
 |         MEMSAL3.TXT
 |         MEMSAL4.TXT
 |
 |---LETTERS
 |         LETSAL1.WRI
 |         LETSAL2.WRI
 |         LETSAL3.WRI
 |         LETSAL4.WRI
 |
ACCOUNTS
 |
 |---MEMOS
 |         MEMACC1.TXT
 |         MEMACC2.TXT
 |         MEMACC3.TXT
 |         MEMACC4.TXT
 |
 |---LETTERS
           LETACC1.WRI
           LETACC2.WRI
           LETACC3.WRI
           LETACC4.WRI
```

Paper exercises (answers in appendix 5)

You are in the root directory, give the DOS command to:

1. Delete all the files in a subdirectory called SALES

2. Delete files in the subdirectory SALES beginning with the characters DST

3. Remove the subdirectory SALES and any files/subdirectories that it contains

4. Print a file in the SALES subdirectory called MAYSALES.A

5. Display the contents of a text file in the root directory JIM.TXT pausing every screenful.

172

Summary of commands

Notes:

Optional elements of commands are shown in square brackets [ ]
Do **not** include these square brackets when you type the command, they are only there to guide you.

Commands may be typed in uppercase or lowercase.

All commands must be followed by pressing the Enter Key.

DELETE [drive:][path] file name

Delete a file

DELTREE [drive:][path] directory name

Remove a directory and any files/directories that it contains

PRINT [drive:][path] file name

Print a file

RD [drive:][path] directory name

Remove a directory

TYPE [drive:][path] file name Display a file's contents on screen

UNDELETE [drive:][path] file name

Undelete a file

XCOPY source [destination] [/s][/e][/m][/a][/d:]

Copies both files and the directory structure – source must include either or a path

/s   copies subdirectories, unless empty

/e following /s   copies empty subdirectories

/m   copies files with the archive attribute set on and then turns the archive attribute off

/a   copies files with the archive attribute set on and keeps the archive attribute set on

/D:date   copies files created or modified on or after this date

173

Checking and managing your system

Introduction

This final unit is aimed at users who want to understand more about the technical aspects of their PC and its operating environment – a grasp of underlying theory can help you to use your PC more effectively and to solve problems for yourself. First a note of caution however, a little knowledge can be very dangerous, especially if it leads to casual and thoughtless tinkering with vital settings. This is never justified – especially on a college machine that is shared with others! In many of these exercises therefore, you will be observing and finding out about your system rather than changing it.

Skills Covered	Activity
Diagnostics – running	3
Disk – checking	1
Disk – defragmenting	1.3
Editor – using	5.4
Main Memory – checking	2
MS-DOS Reports – printing	1.5, 2.2
MS-DOS Reports – saving	1.5
Path – setting	4
System Files – viewing	5

Previous skills required

Starting MS-DOS   (see Units 10 and 11)
Issuing MS-DOS commands

Resources required

Practice disks a and b

Activity 1   Checking a disk

Introduction

The CHKDSK command checks and produces a status report on a disk. It will report on:

a.   The space used up by files and directories on disk, including any hidden system files

b.   Any free space remaining on disk.

c.   Any bad sectors on disk – these are physical imperfections in the disk surface which were detected during its original formatting – see Unit 10,

d.   Any file that is stored as several separate blocks on disk, ie stored non- contiguously. When files are deleted they leave scattered spaces free on the disk, and a new file may be fitted into a number of these spaces. This means that the file takes longer to retrieve from disk. Eventually the files need to be re-organised, particularly for database files where new records are being added and deleted frequently.

e.   Lost files caused by the computer being turned off when files are in use. The CHKDSK command has an /F switch that recovers these lost file units and either releases them as free disk space or converts them back to separate files, which can then be re-combined using the MS-DOS Editor. This feature is only useful for text files, program files cannot be saved and repaired in this way.

1.   Make sure that practice disk b is in the diskette drive, that A is the active drive and that you are in the root directory. In Unit 14, Activity 2 we practised deleting and undeleting files from this disk, so it probably contains non-contiguous blocks.

2.   Issue the command

   CHKDSK A:\SALES*.*

The CHKDSK command searches the SALES subdirectory of your practice diskette and will display a status report such as the following:

```
            Volume Serial Number is 17D3-1960
                  1457664 bytes total disk space
                  512 bytes in 1 hidden files
                  4096 bytes in 7 directories
                  464384 bytes in 64 user files
                  988672 bytes available on disk
                  512 bytes in each allocation unit
                  2847 total allocation units on disk
                  1931 available allocation units on disk
                  655360 total bytes memory
                  537712 bytes free
            A:\SALES\LETSAL1.WRI Contains 2 non-contiguous blocks
            A:\SALES\LETSAL3.WRI Contains 2 non-contiguous blocks
```

The report for your diskette may be slightly different to this. This report shows that two files – LETSAL1.WRI and LETSAL3.WRI are each fragmented across two separate blocks. This is nothing to worry about. You may get the message 'All specified files are contiguous', indicating no fragmented files on disk.

3. **De-fragmenting the files on disk – MS-DOS 6 only**

   DOS 6 provides a DEFRAG command that reorganises fragmented files so that they form contiguous blocks. Before you use this (or any other defragmentation utility) it is a wise precaution to make a backup copy of the disk; the disk directory uses a File Allocation Table to track files and this could become damaged.
   To find out more about the DEFRAG command type HELP DEFRAG The program contains full on-screen help facilities.

4. **The SCANDISK command – MS-DOS 6 only**

   The SCANDISK command can check on and fix a wider range of problems than CHKDSK.
   Try issuing this command, the surface scan can identify imperfections on the disk surface and move data to undamaged areas.

5. **Independent activity**

   The CHKDSK report can be saved to disk and/or printed using the '>' redirection symbol:
   To print the report you end the command with >PRN

   To save the report to A drive in a file called STATUS you would end the command >A:\STATUS

   Produce a CHKDSK report for the ACCOUNTS subdirectory of your diskette, directing it to file and/or printer.

Activity 2   Checking the main memory

Introduction

While the programs or data remain on disk they cannot be used – they must be transferred to main memory. The main memory on your PC is a temporary storage area that holds any programs or data that is currently being used. Main memory is also known as random access memory or RAM, sometimes it is referred to as internal memory to distinguish it from external disk storage.

Some programs, particularly those using Windows, need a lot of memory to run. On new PC's 4 megabytes (4 million characters of information) is regarded as an absolute minimum.

The command MEM allows us to investigate the amount of memory being used, and how much remains free. It also tells you the type of memory used on your PC. If you have a 80386 PC or later then your main memory is probably divided into three main types:

    a.   **Conventional memory.** All PC's have conventional memory; it holds those parts of the operating system that need to be running all the time, eg device driver programs for the keyboard and mouse. The conventional memory that remains is used by other programs. Normally the conventional memory size is only 640k, a limitation left over from earlier versions of DOS. All programs need to use part of conventional memory in order to run.

    b.   **Upper memory area** is 384k of memory space which is reserved for running the system hardware, eg the VDU. Taken with conventional memory they form the 1Mb minimum main memory for a PC. Special programs called memory managers allow part of the upper memory area to be used for device drivers, freeing up conventional memory for more programs.

    c.   **Extended memory.** All the main memory above the 1Mb that is used by a and b above is extended memory. Later versions of DOS use memory managers such as HIMEM.SYS and MEMMAKER to give programs access to extended memory. They are important in reducing the demands made on the limited conventional memory space. If you get an error message reporting insuffient memory it is usually conventional memory.

1.   Type the command **HELP MEM** and you will see that the MEM command can be used either without any parameters or with 3 switches.

    The /C switch is the most informative.

    a.   **MS-DOS Version 5 only.**

       Issue the command MEM/C (the |MORE parameter will pause the scrolling) and a report resembling the following will be displayed:

Conventional Memory :

Name	Size in Decimal		Size in Hex
MSDOS	74704	(73.0K)	123D0
HIMEM	3696	(3.6K)	E70
COMMAND	6496	(6.3K)	1960
KEYB	6208	(6.1K)	1840
MOUSE	16144	(15.8K)	3F10
FREE	64	(0.1K)	40
FREE	96	(0.1K)	60
FREE	547712	(534.9K)	85B80

Total FREE : 547872 (535.0K)

Total bytes available to programs : 547872 (535.0K)

Largest executable program size : 547584 (534.8K)

3145728 bytes total contiguous extended memory

0 bytes available contiguous extended memory

3080192 bytes available XMS memory

64Kb High Memory Area available

b. **MS-DOS Version 6 only**

Issue the command

MEM/C/P

(the /P switch will pause the scrolling) and a report resembling the following will be displayed:

Modules using memory below 1 MB:

Name	Total	=	Conventional	+	Upper Memory
MSDOS	15,565 (15K)		15,565 (15K)		0 (0K)
HIMEM	1,168 (1K)		1,168 (1K)		0 (0K)
EMM386	3,120 (3K)		3,120 (3K)		0 (0K)
COMMAND	2,928 (3K)		2,928 (3K)		0 (0K)
SETVER	512 (1K)		0 (0K)		512 (1K)
DISPLAY	8,336 (8K)		0 (0K)		8,336 (8K)
SMARTDRV	27,488 (27K)		0 (0K)		27,488 (27K)
MOUSE	16,160 (16K)		0 (0K)		16,160 (16K)
KEYB	6,944 (7K)		0 (0K)		6,944 (7K)
Free	731,632 (714K)		632,480 (618K)		99,152 (97K)

Memory Summary:

Type of Memory	Total	=	Used	+	Free
Conventional	655,360		22,880		632,480
Upper	158,592		59,440		99,152
Reserved	393,216		393,216		0
Extended (XMS)	2,987,136		1,270,912		1,716,224

Press any key to continue . . .

Total memory 4,194,304 1,746,448 2,447,856

Total under 1 MB 813,952 82,320 731,632

Largest executable program size 632,384 (618K)

178

Largest free upper memory block   85,648 (84K)

MS-DOS is resident in the high memory area.

The first part of the MEM report is a table showing the programs currently using conventional memory – device drivers for KEYBoard and mouse, plus those parts of MS-DOS currently resident in conventional memory. The third column shows in brackets the amount of memory used in kilobytes.

On my machine 632k of conventional memory remains free to run other programs.

The second part of the report summarises the amount of extended memory free – approximately 1.7 megabytes on my machine.

2. **Independent activity.**(Windows users only) When Windows is running it takes up part of main memory. To find out how much do the following:

   a. Use **MEM/C>PRN** to print off the MEM report.

   b. Start Windows.

   c. On the Main desktop double-click the MS-DOS Prompt icon. You are returned to the MS-DOS prompt, but Windows carries on running in the background.

   Change to A drive again if necessary

   d. Use MEM/C>PRN to print off the MEM report again.

   e. Now compare the two reports. Various Windows programs continue running in the background. How much main memory do they use?

   f. Type EXIT to return to Windows and exit Windows in the usual way.

Activity 3   Checking your hardware (MS-DOS 6 only)

Introduction

MS-DOS 6 offers Microsoft Diagnostics which provides technical information about all aspects of your system, including the hardware. Some are too technical for a publication of this type but others can be used to provide useful supplementary information such as the type of central processing unit, hard disk types and memory.

1. Type the command **MSD** The Microsoft Diagnostics main menu screen appears, showing a general description of your computer – memory disk drives, monitor attached (video) etc.

2. Each of the grey boxes can be selected to provide more detailed information. (use the mouse or the highlighted letter) Try this for some of the options.

3.   At the top of the screen are 3 menus – FIle, Utilities and Help.

Select the **File** menu using the mouse or the Alt key. A number of key system files AUTOEXEC.BAT, CONFIG.SYS etc are listed. These are discussed in more detail in Activity 5.

You have the option of displaying or printing their contents – try this. (not all the files listed may be available on your system)

4.   **Independent activity**

Use MSD to find out:

a.   free space on your main disk drive.

b.   your Windows version.

c.   your processor type.

Exit MSD.

Activity 4   Setting a path

Introduction

We have already learnt that we need to include the correct path when using DOS commands. If we don't tell DOS, eg, the drive and directory where the files that we want to use are stored then the files cannot be used. This is equally true for DOS commands themselves. DOS has two sorts of commands – internal and external. Internal are the most commonly used commands such as DIR and COPY. They are all part of the main DOS command processor program COMMAND.COM. This program is loaded into main memory when the PC starts up so its commands are always available. The less common commands would use up valuable conventional memory if they were always memory resident (see Activity 2) so they are stored as separate programs in the DOS subdirectory. DOS knows where to find these commands because the path is automatically set when the PC starts up. Let's see how.

1.   Change to the C drive and check that you have subdirectory called DOS.

Change to it, using

CD \DOS

Now issue the command

DIR *.EXE/W

– many of the program names are the names of external commands that you have already used, eg CHKDSK, XCOPY, MEM, HELP; typing the program name runs the command.

2.   Now issue the command **PATH** to find out how the path has been set – it will vary depending on how your PC has been set up. On my PC the DOS response is: PATH=C:\WINDOWS;C:\DOS

It instructs DOS, if it cannot find a program file in its current directory, first to look in the Windows directory on C drive, then in the DOS directory on C drive.

3. This path appears as a command in the AUTOEXEC.BAT file – see Activity 5 – and is set every time the PC starts up.
Let's see what happens when the path is not set.

Insert practice disk a in A drive, you will recall that it is a system disk, so can be used to start up the PC.

Turn off the PC, wait a few seconds and turn it on again. The system prompt A> shows.

4. Type **DIR** – this command works as it is an *internal* command.

Type **HELP** – you will get an error message, as the operating system does not know the path to this *external* command. This is because the path has not been set.

Type PATH – you will get the message 'No path'. To reset the path type in the command PATH=C:\WINDOWS;C:\DOS

5. Type HELP again. This time the command works as MS-DOS can locate it in the DOS directory.

6. Remove the practice diskette and start the PC up. This time the path will be correctly set by the path command in the AUTOEXEC.BAT file.

Activity 5   Understanding AUTOEXEC.BAT and CONFIG.SYS files

Introduction

These two files allow you to personally decide how your PC uses its internal resources and how it communicates with its peripherals. These peripherals can be classified into **input** devices, eg keyboard and mouse, and **output** devices, eg monitor and printer. Disk drives are both input and output (i/o) devices as they can be both read from and written to. All these devices have special programs called device drivers that control them. They form part of the operating system; when the computer starts up they are read from disk into main memory. This is the role of the CONFIG.SYS file; as its name suggests it configures the system by:

a. specifying which device drivers to install

b. giving instructions about main memory and file usage.

In this way a PC can be set up to suit the programs that you use and your way of working. When you install a new piece of software usually the installation routine will automatically modify your AUTOEXEC.BAT and CONFIG.SYS files in order to optimise the running of the software.

MS-DOS reads the CONFIG.SYS file into main memory and carries out the commands that it contains. Here's a typical CONFIG.SYS file, yours will differ to some extent, depending on your requirements.

DEVICE=C:\DOS\SETVER.EXE

DEVICE=C:\WINDOWS\HIMEM.SYS

SHELL=COMMAND.COM /P /E:2048

FILES=60

BUFFERS=40

COUNTRY=044,,C:\DOS\COUNTRY.SYS

STACKS=9,256

A brief explanation of each command follows:

DEVICE=C:\DOS\SETVER.EXE

The DEVICE= command loads a device driver, specifying its path. In this case the SETVER.EXE program, located in the DOS directory on C drive, is loaded. This driver allows programs written for earlier versions of DOS to work with later versions.

DEVICE=C:\WINDOWS\HIMEM.SYS

The HIMEM.SYS device driver is one of several possible memory managers your PC may be using. It stops programs using the same parts of extended memory.

SHELL=COMMAND.COM /P /E:2048

The SHELL= command specifies the directory where the MS-DOS command processor COMMAND.COM is located, in this case in the root directory. The switches allow you to fine tune the system further for certain programs.

FILES=60

Allows you to set the maximum number of files open at any one time. Many programs, including Windows, will not work unless the number is 30 or more. Setting the number too high uses up main memory at the expense of space for programs.

BUFFERS=40

A disk buffer is a 512k part of main memory that holds data recently transferred between main memory and disk. If, as is likely, this data will be needed again then it will be immediately available. This will speed up programs requiring a lot of disk activity. As with the FILES command setting the number too high can waste main memory.

COUNTRY=044,,C:\DOS\COUNTRY.SYS

The country command sets the date, time, currency symbol and other conventions to a particular country. 044 is the UK code. The path to the COUNTRY.SYS program is also given.

STACKS=9,256

If you are using Windows it is important to define the number and size of the stacks – these are segments of main memory used for temporary storage.

After executing all the commands in the CONFIG.SYS file DOS will next look for the AUTOEXEC.BAT file and automatically execute the commands that it contains. (hence the name) Typically it is used to run certain programs as soon as the PC starts up. For example if I wish first to run a virus check on the hard disk and then run Windows; I would place appropriate commands in the AUTOEXEC.BAT file.

Here's a typical AUTOEXEC.BAT file; again yours will differ to some extent, depending how your PC has been set up.

```
C:\WINDOWS\SMARTDRV.EXE
PROMPT $p$g
PATH C:\WINDOWS;C:\DOS
KEYB UK
SET TEMP=C:\WINDOWS\TEMP
CD\MOUSE
MOUSE
```

A brief explanation of each command follows:

```
C:\WINDOWS\SMARTDRV.EXE
```

SMARTDRV.EXE is a disk-caching program, in this case stored in the Windows subdirectory. A disk cache is an area of main memory that stores the most recently used information. When it is next needed it can be accessed in main memory which is much faster than reading it from disk, thus speeding up the computer's processing time. The most recent versions of the SMARTDRV program will automatically set up the cache size.

```
PROMPT $p$g
```

This has already been explained in Unit 11, Activity 1. It sets up the standard MS-DOS prompt, consisting of the drive letter and the current directory.

```
PATH C:\WINDOWS;C:\DOS
```

This has already been explained in Activity 4. By including the path in the AUTOEXEC.BAT file the operating system will look in the DOS then the WINDOWS subdirectories for any commands that it cannot find in the current directory. Notice that a semicolon separates each path. If you include too many directories in the PATH command it will slow down the PC, as every time you type an incorrect command DOS will search the path specified, trying to locate it.

```
KEYB UK
```

KEYB UK loads the memory resident UK keyboard program – see Activity 2.

SET TEMP=C:\WINDOWS\TEMP

Many Windows-based programs create temporary files while they are running in order to store data. This command designates a directory to hold them called TEMP, located in the WINDOWS subdirectory.

CD\MOUSE

This changes to the mouse subdirectory

MOUSE

This loads the memory-resident program MOUSE.EXE that controls the mouse. If this program were not run the mouse would not work.

Note: Some of the above commands may be preceded by LH. The LOADHIGH command saves conventional memory space by loading programs into the upper memory area

Now that you have a general idea what these two essential files do we will try modifying a copy of the AUTOEXEC.BAT file. It would be extremely unwise to edit the original so we will copy them to your system diskette, practice disk a.

1. Locate the directory that contains the AUTOEXEC.BAT and CONFIG.SYS files. It is probably the root directory or the DOS subdirectory. If not change to the root directory on C drive and use DIR *.BAT /S and DIR *.SYS /S to locate them.

2. Now insert your system diskette, practice disk a and change to A drive – *this is very important.*

   Assuming that these files are located in the root directory of C drive the commands to copy them to your practice disk would be:

   COPY C:\AUTOEXEC.BAT A: and

   COPY C:\CONFIG.SYS A:

   If they are in a subdirectory then this must be included in the path.

3. Issue the command

   EDIT A:\AUTOEXEC.BAT

   Make sure that you include the path A: in the command.

   The MS-DOS Editor screen appears, with the AUTOEXEC.BAT file, ready to be edited.

   Troubleshooting. If the editor screen is blank then you have probably spelt the name of the file incorrectly. In this case DOS assumes that you wish to create a new file of that name.

   You need to exit and re-issue the command correctly.

   Mouse method. Move the screen cursor – a coloured square – onto the File menu and click the left mouse button. The menu opens.

   Move the cursor onto the Exit option and left-click the mouse button.

Keyboard method. Press the Alt then the Down Arrow key to open the File Menu.

Use the Down Arrow key to select the Exit option, then press the Enter key.

4. **The Editor screen.** The MS-DOS Editor operates in a similar way to many word and text processors. You have already used it to create your sample files.

   Menus. If you have a mouse you move the screen cursor – a coloured square – onto the File menu and and click the left mouse button. The menu opens.

   The menus can also be selected by pressing the Alt key, then using the arrow keys and the Enter key to select an option.

   Inserting a line. Move the cursor to the start of a line and press the Enter key.

   Deleting a line. Move the cursor to the beginning of a line and press the Delete key until the text is deleted.

   Inserting text. Position the cursor and start typing!

   Deleting text. Position the cursor and use the Delete or the Backspace key.

   Scroll bars. You may find that the text disappears off the screen. If so you can use the arrow keys or the scroll bars to re-position the text.

5. **Editing the AUTOEXEC.BAT File**

   Move the cursor to the end of the file and create a new line. Add the command DATE

   Now add the command TIME on a new line.

   (if you already have these commands in your file then go on to section 8)

6. Now open the **File** menu and select the **Save** option (not SAVE as)

   Open the **File** menu again and select **Exit.**

   You are returned to the DOS prompt.

7. Type AUTOEXEC

   This runs the AUTOEXEC.BAT file. You can now see the effect of these changes. DOS prompts you to check the date and time.

   Note: AUTOEXEC is a batch file (see Activity 6) that can be run any time. To see the effect of any changes to CONFIG.SYS the PC would need to be be re-started.

8. **Independent activity**

   Edit the AUTOEXEC.BAT file on the *practice disk again.*

   Add the command DOSKEY to the end of the file.

185

Save this change and run the file again.

You will remember that DOSKEY is a memory-resident program that stores previously issued commands for re-use. Press the Up Arrow key to test this.

Summary of commands

Notes:

Optional elements of commands are shown in square brackets [ ]

Do **not** include these square brackets when you type the command, they are only there to guide you.

Commands may be typed in uppercase or lowercase.

All commands must be followed by pressing the Enter Key

CHKDSK [drive:][path] [/f]	Checks the status of a disk – see Activity 1, the /f switch fixes disk errors
DEFRAG [drive:]	Reorganises fragmented files on disk
SCANDISK [drive:]	Checks disk for a wide range of errors
MEM [/c]	Reports on main memory used and free, the /c switch shows programs currently running in memory
MSD (DOS 6 only)	Runs Microsoft Diagnostics program
PATH [drive:]path1;path2;etc	Sets the search path for executable files, eg MS-DOS, Windows.
EDIT [drive:][path][file name]	Use MS-DOS text editor

Batch files and viruses

Introduction

In this Unit you will be creating batch files to disolay a user menu, you will also be using the MS-DOS anti virus application. (MS-DOS 6 only)

Skills Covered   **Activity**

Batch File – creating   1
Viruses – checking for   2

Previous skills required

Starting MS-DOS   (see Units 10 and 11)
Issuing MS-DOS commands

Resources required

Practice disks a and b.

Activity 1   Creating simple batch files

Introduction

1. A batch file is a text file used to store a series of MS-DOS commands. Typing the name of the file (plus Enter) causes the stored commands to be executed one after the other, ie in a batch. Some of the commands are ordinary MS-DOS commands that you have already used, others can only be used in batch files. A batch file is in effect a short program instructing the computer to carry out a series of operations.

    Batch files must have the extension .BAT, the AUTOEXEC.BAT file that you edited in Unit 15, Activity 5 is a special type of batch file as it is automatically executed when MS-DOS starts up.

2. Say that you want to copy files from one diskette to another. The command XCOPY A: B: will do this but involves a lot of tedious disk swopping – see Unit 13 Activity 3.

187

Below is an example of a short batch file that performs this task. It copies files from the diskette to a temporary directory TEMPCOPY on C drive, then copies the contents of this directory to the backup disk. When copying is complete the temporary directory and its contents are deleted from C drive:

```
CLS
ECHO  INSERT THE DISK YOU WISH TO COPY IN DRIVE A
C:
CD\
MD TEMPCOPY
COPY A:*.* C:\TEMPCOPY
ECHO  INSERT BACKUP DISK IN DRIVE A
PAUSE
COPY C:\TEMPCOPY\*.* A:
CD \TEMPCOPY
DEL *.*
CD\
RD \TEMPCOPY
ECHO COPYING COMPLETE, PLEASE REMOVE BACKUP DISK
```

Notes: The command CLS clears the screen; the special batch file command ECHO displays user messages on the screen, and PAUSE halts the execution of the batch file until a key is pressed.

3. In using batch files like this one you can:

   a. save time – the batch file, once created, can be used repeatedly. There is no need to type the individual commands each time.

   b. automate tasks of particular relevance to you.

4. If you use a mix of DOS and Windows applications, as many users do, then you can create a batch file that offers a menu of choices, eg:

   USER MENU

   A.   USE MS-DOS HELP

   B.   CHECK DATE

   C.   CHECK TIME

   D.   USE WINDOWS

   PLEASE MAKE CHOICE AND PRESS ENTER

You will be developing this menu and learning how to extend it and adapt it for your own applications.

1. Insert your system diskette a in A drive and make sure that A is the current drive.

2. We will use the MS-DOS editor to create our batch files. (any text or word processor capable of creating an ASCII text file will do, including Windows Notepad)

   Issue the command **EDIT A:\ MENU.BAT**

   The MS-DOS editor screen appears (Unit 15 Activity 5 contains instructions how to use it)

3. Create the following batch file; when you have finished, save it and exit from the Editor.

   ```
   @ECHO OFF
   CLS
   ECHO
   ECHO
   ECHO     USER MENU
   ECHO
   ECHO
   ECHO     A. USE MS-DOS HELP
   ECHO
   ECHO     B. CHECK DATE
   ECHO.
   ECHO     C. CHECK TIME
   ECHO
   ECHO     D. USE WINDOWS
   ECHO
   ECHO
   ```

   Notes: The ECHO command displays the text message that follows it on screen.

   ECHO. inserts a blank line on screen to produce a neater display.

   The command @ECHO OFF stops the batch file commands themselves appearing on screen, ie the words CLS and ECHO. It is good idea not to include @ECHO OFF until you have tested the batch file; in case of problems the commands echoed on screen show you which commands were executed.

   When you have finished, save it and exit from the Editor.

4. Now run the batch file by typing MENU – it should display the menu title and the four choices on screen.

Troubleshooting.

a. Check that you have used the .BAT extension, otherwise MS-DOS will not recognise it as a batch file. Use the REN command to rename it if necessary.

b. If the display is incorrect issue the command EDIT A:\ MENU.BAT again and check the spelling and syntax of the commands used.

5. Now that we have the menu display working we need to write batch files to run the four options displayed – A. USE MS-DOS HELP, B. CHECK DATE etc.

   DOS 6 Users: If you are using DOS 6 you may prefer to use the interactive program in section 10 below, which tests the option that the user keys in – A, B, C, D etc. In earlier versions of DOS a batch file program cannot do this, it is simply a series of commands that execute one after the other. Instead we will have to write four smaller programs A.BAT, B.BAT, C.BAT and D.BAT for each option. This works quite well – except that when the user presses the wrong key they get a DOS error message.

6. Let's create the first batch file. Issue the command **EDIT A:\ A.BAT**

   The MS-DOS editor screen appears. Enter the commands:

       @ECHO OFF
       REM MENU OPTION A – CALLS UP HELP
       HELP
       MENU

   When you have finished, save it and exit from the Editor.

7. Now run the batch file by typing A (plus Enter)

   The action is very simple:

   The DOS command HELP runs Help.

   When the user exits from Help the command MENU runs the MENU.BAT batch file to display the menu options again. (nb one batch file can call another)

   The REM command places a remark in the program to remind you of its purpose. You can use as many remarks as you need without affecting the running of the program. REM is also useful when you are testing batch files to temporarily disable a command – insert REM at the start of the command and it is ignored.

   Troubleshooting

   I am assuming that the PATH command in the AUTOEXEC.BAT file includes the DOS directory – see Unit 15, Activity 4. Check this by typing PATH
   If it does not then you will need to include a command in the batch file to change to the DOS directory, eg CD \DOS before the HELP command. This will also apply to the date and time options.

8. Independent activities

a. Create the two batch files B.BAT and C.BAT to display the date and time – merely follow the model of A.BAT, but include the DATE and TIME commands instead. Run these batch files to test them.

b. Now create the batch file D.BAT to run Windows – if of course Windows is installed on your machine! First check that the Windows is included in the path – see the Troubleshooting section above. If so you will merely need include the command WIN - this runs the main Windows program WIN.EXE. Otherwise you will have to include the command to change to the Windows subdirectory.

Type D to test this option; Windows should start up.

Exit Windows and the menu should be re-displayed. The batch file remains active when you are running Windows, when Windows ends DOS executes the next command in the batch file, MENU which re-displays the menu.

Note: This batch file will not run if Windows is already running in the background, make sure that you have exited to DOS.

c. Now let's extend the menu to add other applications that you have on your PC, eg a word processor or spreadsheet. First you need to add the options to the batch file MENU.BAT

Issue the command EDIT A:\ MENU.BAT and add the options, eg

      ECHO
      ECHO E.   USE WINDOWS PAINT
      ECHO
      ECHO F.   USE WORDPERFECT FOR DOS

Now you must create the batch files to run these applications as before, ie E.BAT and F.BAT.

Hints

a. Paint is part of Windows so you can run Windows and the application in the one command, **WIN PBRUSH** (WIN runs Windows and PBRUSH runs the program PBRUSH.EXE)

If you wish to run a Windows-based application such as the Excel spreadsheet first check the path (see trouble shooting section above) Does the path include Excel?

If so you can run Windows and the application using the command, WIN EXCEL

If not then you will need to include the path in the command, eg:

      WIN C:\EXCEL\EXCEL

Use the same principle for any Windows-based application that you choose.

b. To run a non-Windows, ie a DOS-based application you first need to find out the name of the directory where the application is stored and the name of the main program (.EXE) file. This is usually straightforward.

Change to the root directory of the drive holding the application and use the TREE command to find the directory, in the case of eg Wordperfect for DOS it is probably WP

Then locate the .EXE file using the DIR command, eg DIR \WP*.EXE

In the case of Wordperfect it is WP.EXE

So your batch file would be:

```
@ECHO OFF
REM MENU OPTION F CALLS UP WORDPERFECT
C:
CD\WP
WP
A:
MENU
```

9. The final step is to have the menu displed when your PC starts up. This merely entails editing the AUTOEXEC.BAT file and adding the command MENU to the end. *Do this to the copy on your system disk (not the one on C drive).*

10. **DOS 6 Only – the choice command.** DOS 6 includes a CHOICE command which can test the user's choice of menu option. This allows for one batch file program to handle all the options rather than using a separate batch file for each option.

Look at the following batch file MENU2.BAT:

```
@ECHO OFF
CLS
ECHO
ECHO
ECHO      USER MENU
ECHO
ECHO
ECHO      A. USE MS-DOS HELP
ECHO.
ECHO      B. CHECK DATE
ECHO
ECHO      C. CHECK TIME
ECHO.
ECHO      D. USE WINDOWS
ECHO
```

192

```
ECHO        E. EXIT MENU
ECHO
ECHO
CHOICE /C:ABCDE ENTER A LETTER
IF ERRORLEVEL 5 GOTO EXIT
IF ERRORLEVEL 4 GOTO WINDOWS
IF ERRORLEVEL 3 GOTO TIME
REM ADD MORE TESTS FOR OPTION A, B ETC HERE
:WINDOWS
WIN
GOTO END
:TIME
TIME
GOTO END
:END
MENU2
:EXIT
```

11. **Explanation of the program**

Look at the second part of the program, shown in bold, it is in four parts:

CHOICE /C:ABCD ENTER A LETTER Places the prompt ENTER A LETTER on screen and offers choices A, B, C and D.

IF ERRORLEVEL....GOTO.... can be rather misleading. ERROR-LEVEL does not only test for errors. In this case every choice the user keys in – A, B, C, or D returns a number called an exit code to DOS. Notice that they are tested in reverse order as DOS tests for the code being greater or equal to a specific number.

The GOTO command jumps to another part of the program identified by a label (a line beginning with a colon), the commands following the label are then executed. So, eg, GOTO WINDOWS skips the next 2 lines to the label :WINDOWS. The WIN command following the label then runs Windows.

When the WIN command is executed control returns to the batch file. The final command after each label is GOTO END. The program then goes to the :END label and the command MENU2 runs the batch file again and displays the menu.

12. **Independent activity**

Create the above batch file MENU2.BAT on your diskette and test it. Remember that a batch file can be cancelled by pressing the Ctrl and C keys.

Modify it to run the other 2 options DATE and HELP – you will find the help text for the CHOICE command offers useful guidance/examples.

Activity 2   Checking for viruses. (MS-DOS 6 only)

Introduction

The first computer viruses appeared on PC's in the 1980's. There are now several thousand viruses in circulation. They can spread, often unnoticed, and pose a serious threat to any computer system. Organisations have been compelled to establish anti-virus measures to combat the threat. A computer virus is a small program that spreads by attaching itself to another program on disk. The infected program may attack a COM or EXE file, or the boot sector of the disk. (this stores instructions so that the operating system can start to read or 'boot' the disk)

When the infected program is run the virus looks for other programs to infect.

Despite scare stories in the media most viruses are merely nuisances, displaying strange messages or making the system behave oddly. Some however can corrupt or destroy data by eg, formatting disks or deleting files. Viruses are usually spread through organisations by using an infected diskette brought from home or another infected site. Many businesses and colleges now forbid the use of diskettes brought from outside, because of the high cost of removing even a relatively harmless virus.

Virus checking software has the almost impossible task of recognising the new viruses and variants that are emerging all the time. The most common method is to scan the suspect disk for *recognition strings* – a series of bytes that occur in known viruses, but not in a harmless program. Another detection method is the checksum. This performs a mathematical calculation based on the bytes of data in each file and stores the result. A virus will modify the size of the file it infects and the checksum will detect this if run again.

You usually have the options to schedule automatic virus scans at regular intervals or to have the the program permanently running in the background – this saves you having to remember to run the anti-virus program.

MS-DOS 6 provides the Microsoft Antivirus program MSAV. Your version may well be out of date unless you subscribe to the update service and will not be as comprehensive as market leaders such as Norton or Dr Solomons. We will use it to try out some of the anti-virus features.

1. Type the command MSAV and the main menu screen for the Microsoft Antivirus program appears. It offers 5 options – Detect, Detect and Clean, Select New Drive etc.

Use the mouse or the function keys – F1, F2, F3 etc – to select an option.

2. Select the first option, **Detect.** All the files in all directories of the current disk are scanned. The top left corner of the screen shows which file is currently being scanned.

    When complete a report is displayed, showing the number and type of files scanned. If your disk is free of viruses then columns 3 and 4 should show no infected files.

    Select the **OK** button.

3. Take the third option, **Select new drive.** A list of drives is shown in the top left hand corner of the screen.

    Insert practice disk a in the machine and select the appropriate drive letter. The work drive should now show A, B etc.

    Take the **Detect** option again to scan the diskette for viruses.

4. From the Main Menu screen press the **F9** function key. A list of all the viruses recognised by MSAV is displayed. Use the scroll bar or the PgDn key to scroll through the list.

    Find out more about some of the viruses – select the name and then the **Info** button.

    Return to the Main Menu.

5. **Independent activity.** Use the Help option to find out about stealth viruses and checksums on the Options menu.

6. Exit from MSAV.

Summary of commands

Notes:

Optional elements of commands are shown in square brackets [ ]
Do **not** include these square brackets when you type the command, they are only there to guide you.

Commands may be typed in uppercase or lowercase.

All commands must be followed by pressing the Enter Key

Ctrl – C Cancel a batch file while running

Batch file commands. The following commands can only be used in batch files, not typed at the MS-DOS Prompt.

CHOICE [C:keys] [message]	Pauses batch file and offers user a choice, C: specifies optional keys to press, and a message can be added as a prompt
@ECHO OFF	Stops batch file commands being displayed when executing
ECHO.	Display a blank line on screen
ECHO [text]	Display a line of text on screen
GOTO :label name	Sends DOS to a line in a batch file marked by a label. A label can be up to 8 characters and begin with a colon (:)
IF ERRORLEVELnumber	Tests for an exit code greater than or equal to a particular number
REM	Insert a remark in a batch file

196

Appendices

Appendix 1

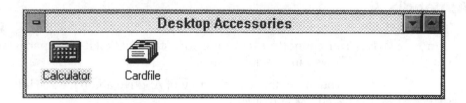

Appendix 2

BUDGET.1	Valid
JUNEBUDGET.1	Invalid - name exceeds 8 characters
ACCN_MAY	Valid
ACCN\MAY.WRK	Invalid ' \ ' character
MEMBERS.DBF1	Invalid - extension must not exceed 3 characters
MEMBERS.DBF	Valid
APR SLS.XLS	Invalid - spaces not allowed in file names

Appendix 3

3a. DIR \WINDOWS*.HLP /ON/P lists all the files in the WINDOWS directory with extension .HLP in alphabetic order, pausing every screenful

3b. DIR *.?C? /S lists all files with C as the 2nd character of the extension, searching all subdirectories

3c. In a, DIR is the command name, \WINDOWS\ the path name, *.HLP the file name and /ON/P the switches.

3d. In the command DIR /DOS/*.COM \W the three slash characters are the wrong way round.

4a. If you are in the root directory the command you would give to change to the the SYSTEM subdirectory of the WINDOWS subdirectory is CD \WINDOWS\SYSTEM

4b. The command which changes from the SYSTEM subdirectory to the DOS subdirectory is CD \DOS

4c. CD\ always returns you to the root directory

4d. If you are in the root directory the command you would you give to display the directory tree for the WINDOWS subdirectory, including its files, sending it to the printer is

TREE/A/F \WINDOWS>PRN

Appendix 4

1. You cannot create a directory called MY FILES - spaces are not allowed in directory names.

2. If you are in the root directory of A: drive and have 2 subdirectories called JIM and JOHN.

   The command to copy:

   a. All files with the extension .TXT from JIM to JOHN is

      COPY \JIM*.* \JOHN

   b. All files with beginning in OLD from the root directory to JIM is

      COPY OLD*.* \JIM

3. The unnecessary elements in the following command are shown in bold:

   COPY A:\JOHN\BUDGET.1 **A:\JIM\BUDGET.1**

Appendix 5

If you are in the root directory the DOS command to:

1. delete all the files in a subdirectory called SALES is DEL SALES*.*

2. delete files in the subdirectory SALES beginning with the characters DST is

   DEL SALES\DST*.*

3. remove the subdirectory SALES and any files/subdirectories that it contains is

   DELTREE SALES

4. print a file in the SALES subdirectory called MAYSALES.A is

   PRINT SALES\MAYSALES.A

5. display the contents of a text file in the root directory JIM.TXT, pausing every screenful is TYPE JIM.TXT|MORE

Index